Titbits
and Tales
of Essex Inns

by Mavis Sipple

Published by Brent Publications 2001
Fleet House, Benfleet, Essex SS7 4FH
ISBN No. 0 948706 12 0
The material in this book is copyright and may not be reproduced
by any means without the specific permission of the author.

Printed by Basildon Printing Company Limited
Fleet House, Armstrong Road, Benfleet, Essex SS7 4FH

CONTENTS

INTRODUCTION	V
ASHINGDON	1
BENFLEET	2
BILLERICAY	6
BLACKMORE	12
BRAINTREE	13
BULPHAN	15
CANEWDON	17
CANVEY ISLAND	20
CLACTON	24
COGGLESHALL	26
COLCHESTER	28
DUNMOW	31
FAMBRIDGE	33
FOBBING	36
FOULNESS	38
FRINTON ON SEA	40
GREAT LEIGHS	42
HARWICH	43
HEMPSTEAD	45
HOCKLEY	47
HORNDON ON THE HILL	51
LEIGH ON SEA	53
MALDON	63
PAGLESHAM	64
PELDON	67
ROCHFORD	71
SHOEBURYNESS	76
STAPLEFORD TAWNEY	77
STOCK	79
TILBURY	82
WAKERING	84
WALTHAM ABBEY	86
WOODHAM MORTIMER	87

Front Cover Pictures
The Punchbowl, Paglesham
The Woolpack, Coggleshall

Back Cover Pictures
Welsh Harp, Waltham Abbey
The Hurdlemakers Arms, Woodham Mortimer

INTRODUCTION

DURING the Middle Ages most ordinary people did not venture far from their own village. The majority of those travelling on the roads were either pilgrims going to worship at an important shrine, or monks going from monastery to monastery. They lodged in the priories or monasteries where food, drink and a bed for the night were always available. Gradually, more and more people began to journey around the country and the monasteries were unable to cope with the great demand for accommodation. Thus the first hotels came into being. Later they were run independently of the monasteries.

As very few people could read and write at that time, the hotels put out picture signs. Often a bell or bull (from boule being the name of the seal of a monastery). If there were several inns in one area they needed different signs. Most of them still kept to a religious theme such as The Angel, The Monk's Head or The Crusader.

Some innkeepers took on part of the Arms of the local Lord of the Manor for their sign. Names like The Bear, The Lion, or The Dragon. Others, to show their loyalty to the monarch chose The Crown, Royal Oak, or the King's Arms. The Sun and Moon are thought to refer to the pagan gods Apollo and Diana, while The Fox and Hounds or the White Hart have links with the sporting activities in the area. These days, signs are very diverse in name and meaning. The Invisible Man, The Kicking Dickey, The Hobgoblin are fairly obscure names, whereas some have local connections such as The Catcracker at Stanford le Hope which takes its name from a process used at the nearby oil refineries at Coryton or the Last Post which was once the main Post Office in Southend.

Inn signs are by no means a modern idea. They were used as far back as Roman times, when a green bush was used as an advertisement. At one time ale was brewed and sold from hundreds of cottages throughout the country. A bush had to be hung outside to show that ale was on sale. Ale was drunk by nearly everyone. It was easy to make, reasonably cheap and more hygienic than much of the water that was available. Even the Church made money from the sale of beer. If they were short of funds to buy new furnishings or to repair the roof they would organise an Aleing, a kind of church fair, perhaps the beginnings of the church fete. These Aleings would be quite an event, everyone took part and made merry, often for several days. The Aleing finished when enough money had been raised.

As early as the 1300's the selling of ale was strictly controlled, it was an offence to sell beer at more, or at less than one penny per gallon. Alehouses were invariably run by wives while the husband worked at some other trade. By 1552 no alehouse could be opened without a licence granted by two Justices of the Peace. Every victualler and alehouse keeper had to find two people to stand surety at a cost of £5 for one year. Publicans were required by law to hang out a sign. The law stated *'whosoever shall brew ales in the town with the intention of selling it, must hang out a sign or forfeit his ale.'* All those named were licensed to *'keep the trade of victualling and keeping of common alehouse.'* They were permitted to *'brew and bake that which shall be wholesome, not to support any offenders, vagabonds or ill rule keepers.'* They were not to play unlawful games and not allowed to serve food or drink at the time when services were taking place in the church or on the Sabbath day. They were also obliged to keep at least one bed ready for strangers. They were not permitted to turn anyone away.

You can contact Mavis Sipple on 01702 531780

ASHINGDON

The Victory

Ashingdon's main claim to fame is the great battle that is supposed to have taken place there in 1016, when the Danish Canute fought the English on Ashingdon Hill. The victory went to Canute who became King.

Another victory claimed at Ashingdon was the Battle of the Pub. Until 1933 Ashingdon had no pub at all, just an off licence run for ten years by a Mrs Turner. Mrs Turner sold it to Mrs Oscroft who decided to pull down the off licence and build a pub on the opposite side of the road. There was a great deal of council opposition to this plan. but Mrs Oscroft, who had had *'many years experience in the trade and had never had any adverse reports,'* was determined. She said that there was no inn for six miles and one would be beneficial to the local area. She produced a petition signed by six hundred people supporting her, from the folk of Ashingdon and Hawkwell and, even from the Rector. Eventually she was granted a five and a half year licence on condition that food was always available, sandwiches, cheese, bread and butter.

So the pub was built. The sign outside depicts a sailing ship, assumed to be Nelson's Victory. But truly the sign Victory was chosen as tribute to the people of Ashingdon and their determined efforts to have their own Local. It was the *'Victory of the people of Ashingdon,'* and the defeat of the local council.

BENFLEET

The Hoy and Helmet,

According to the deeds, the ancient Hoy and Helmet, South Benfleet, used to be called just The Hoy. Being close to the Thames it was named The Hoy after the flat-bottomed boats used for carrying cargoes to and from London. These hoys were brought into the country by the Dutch settlers who came to nearby Canvey Island during the 1600's to build the sea walls. The Helmet part of the name came around 1923 and is probably named after the mud bank or hard near the inn. The original building dates from the 15th century. The northern part was added during the 18th century.

Builders working on the Hoy and Helmet during the early thirties made some finds that more or less confirm the idea that the inn stands on the site of an ancient Nunnery. They discovered an enormous 14th century fireplace. The stone had been covered over with layers of bricks and plaster. A dividing wall had been built making one large room into two smaller ones, this wall divided the great fireplace into two. Several curved beams were also found. These are similar to those found in other nunneries of the time. They found half a dozen tiny rooms there which are thought to have been cells for the nuns. These were demolished during the work. Workmen also found a secret underground passage leading to the nearby ancient church. It is thought that this was a smuggler's tunnel. Masonry similar to that used to build the old church was also discovered.

Proprietor Jack Phillips advertised the inn as the oldest in Essex, where Lukers ales and stouts, wines, spirits and cigars of the finest quality were available. He invited the public to *'come and see the noted 11th century fireplace.'*

The Half Crown

Standing almost opposite the Hoy & Helmet is The Half Crown. The deeds of this inn go back to 1738.

It was originally a thatched inn named the Crown but in 1786 became a private house. The building was taken down and brick built tenements were put there in its place. Rebuilding was completed again in 1820.

The Crown was renamed the Half Crown when a lorry, which had problems with its brakes at the traffic lights which used to be on the hill, rolled back and demolished part of the building.

The publican held a competition for members of the public to find a suitable name for the pub when it had been repaired. The enterprising winner came up with the name Half Crown.

The sign outside shows both sides of an old half crown coin with the head of George Vl and the date 1937, the year after he was crowned King.

It is in the conservation area of South Benfleet leading to the station.

The Anchor

The Anchor at South Benfleet was built in 1380. At one time it was known as the Blue Anchor. Probably because of all the shipbuilding in the area at the time. The wood was taken from the trees in nearby Shipwrights Wood. The Blue Anchor belonged for a time to John Brewitt. He was a farmer in Benfleet. The Brewitt's were a well-known and respected family of the area. Their name is inscribed on one of the bells in the parish church. Many of the family were buried there including John's two wives, Mary and Ann and also his mother.

In 1875 it was taken over by George Land. Trade was brisk that day, he took £1.16s. for two gallons of Irish whiskey, £1.12s. for two gallons of rum, £8.8s. for four barrels of beer.

When workmen were putting in a new window in the late 1920s, they uncovered a huge ancient arch made of rough hewn oak. It ran between the inner and outer walls and was bolted to the outer wall with massive ties. The innkeeper, Edward Land, was convinced that the inn stands on the sight of an ancient Monastery. At the back of the building are the remains of a moat.

The inn is also thought to stand on the site of a fortified Danish camp. Until 1895 the wells at the Anchor and The Hoy provided the only water available in the village.

The Bread & Cheese

The Bread and Cheese was named after the hill on which it is built. No one really knows the origin of the name.

Some say it is where the workmen sat to eat their lunch of bread and cheese, others that the old name for the hawthorn bushes that grow all along the roadside there, is bread and cheese. The leaves being the bread and the berries the cheese.

There is another theory that at the time of the Wat Tyler rebellion a group of protesters went to Southend and stopped on the hill near South Benfleet. Anyone travelling on the road they thought might be a foreigner was taken to the leaders and made to say bread and cheese. If they were English they could pronounce the words perfectly and were allowed to go on their way, but if they could not pronounce the words correctly it was assumed that they were French and they were hanged from a nearby tree.

BILLERICAY

The Red Lion

The Red Lion is one of Billericay's oldest buildings. At one time it was a private house named Merchants, possibly owned by one of the wealthy Flemish merchants who lived in Billericay. There has been an inn on the site since 1593 when Jacob Warne was tenant of a house called the Lion.

The Red Lion was Headquarters of the Court Leet, under Lord Petre. Court Leet was a court of justice held from the time of Edward the First, it was responsible for making sure the Frank Pledge for good behaviour was kept. The court took place during Whitsun week when various officers such as Ale Taster and Constable were appointed. The last three days were taken up with feasting and making merry.

In the mid 1600's Abraham Thresher of the Red Lion and four other tradesmen from Billericay issued their own tokens. The smallest official coin was the silver penny, there was very little copper coinage. Some enterprising tradespeople issued tokens so that their customers could obtain change. The Threshers were a well known and respected family in the area. The next landlord was Samuel Thresher who also owned the Royal Oak, and several other properties in the area

Another Abraham Thresher of the Red Lion advertised in a Chelmsford newspaper that he had lately set up a very neat and genteel Post Chariot. He humbly hoped the Ladies and Gentlemen in the neighbourhood would favour him with their commands. He assured them that they could depend on being accommodated with able horses and a careful driver to any part of England and their favours would be gratefully acknowledged by their most humble servant.

Several owners later, in 1835, Richard Mumford, agent for the London Corporation Fire and Life Insurance Co. advertised the Red Lion as a Commercial Inn where Post Horses, close and open carriages, flys and gigs could be hired. By 1881 Thomas Sides lived at the Red Lion with his wife, three daughters, his nephew and two domestic servants.

An article in a local newspaper describes how nearly two hundred workers from London visited the inn to partake the good fare provided by Mr Sides. The locals were horrified at the behaviour of the visitors. They went into gardens, stole flowers and fruit and tore down the trees. They went into the reading room, threw books about and threatened to break into the library. One man went through the town carrying a bunch of stinging nettles, which he pushed into people's faces. The law arrived to try to quell the disorder, but the revellers finally 'got clear away.'

Many clubs held their meetings in the Red Lion. The Royal Ancient Order of Buffaloes met there and the 'Sparrow and Rat Club' which at the AGM in 1904 boasted that members had destroyed over three thousand sparrow's eggs. The Red Lion has had many licensees and seen many changes. With the decline of the Coaching trade, part of the Inn was made into a private residence.

According to the Guinness Book of Records, the name The Red Lion is the most common of all pub names.

The Rising Sun

The Rising Sun was built around the eighteenth century but there was a building on the site in 1593. In a Bill of Sale dated 1830 it is described as being well situated where carriages and bicycle traffic must pass. It was an important Coaching House described as being situated at the entrance to the town of Billericay on the busy crossroads to London, Chelmsford and Tilbury Fort. Coaches left for London every morning and Southend every evening. The building consisted of a large parlour, kitchen, scullery, pantry and tiled coalhouse. A coachhouse, cart lodge, timber and tiled four stalled stable and brick stable for four horses with loft. There was also a tiled skittle shed. There were two parlours, a bar, taproom, six bedrooms on the first floor and two on the second. There was also a soldiers room. A small part of the land had been let for £50 a year, The property was sold to Mr. Lambirth for £1,200.

The soldiers room was for use of the troops billeted there, and in several inns and cottages in the area, during the wars with the French. The soldiers were not very welcome guests, constantly fighting and generally misbehaving. The innkeepers in desperation wrote to the Crown to complain about the 'daring insults and inconveniences' they had suffered at the hands of over ten thousand troops and nearly two thousand horses over the past six months. They felt they should be given some compensation. Finally they were awarded £50. This seemed satisfactory to the innkeepers who stated they were satisfied and drank to 'the health of His Majesty'. They added that they wished the troops every success.

Many alterations have taken place over the years; the three bars are now one.

The Railway

It is thought that there was a small inn named the Orange Tree standing right in the path of the proposed Railway. This had to be pulled down and the present Railway Inn was built to take its place. This was finished in 1885. On the outside wall of the building is a tile decorated with the branch of a tree complete with oranges and the date 1885.

There is another theory that it took over from the old Dog and Partridge beerhouse which was run by Ephraim Theobold who was also a marine store dealer.

By 1894, the inn was run by George Bull and later William Bull. William's father, also William, was a local carrier, taking goods, passengers and post to and from Brentwood. The passenger service later became a taxi and car hire service, the only one in the area at the time. This was taken over by Collier's Car Hire Service which for many years ran its business from the yard of the Railway. Outside, the garages which gradually became derelict have recently been tastefully renovated and a big old mangle has been hoisted onto the roof. Inside the pub is cosy and very friendly. It is owned by Grays Brewery, one of the few remaining friendly caring family run breweries.

The White Hart

There has been a White Hart in Billericay since the beginning of the seventeenth century. In 1667 it belonged to Joseph Fishpoole, who was a well known wool merchant. He owned several pieces of land in the area, some of it was used as a hop garden. The present red brick building is not nearly so old, being built in the middle of the eighteenth century. Horse drawn carts are said to have come from Leigh-on-Sea carrying their load of cockles and fish and often the illicit keg of liquor which would be hidden under the cargo until the horses were being looked after at the nearby blacksmith's. Then it would be taken out and dropped down the chute into the White Hart's cellar. Smuggling was part of life in those days.

Like many inns The White Hart was a favourite venue for cock fights, cricket matches, and card schools. One unfortunate servant who had been sent to Billericay Fair to buy some livestock lost eighty pounds to the card sharps and twenty pounds to a pickpocket when he stopped off there for a drink. A newspaper from 1776 tell that a cricket match was to be played at the White Hart Billericay between eleven picked Gentlemen of Barstable against eleven of Billericay, for eleven Gold Laced Hats.

In 1825 when the tenant was William Cornell, the property was auctioned. It had 'two parlours, seven bedrooms two garrets, a brewhouse and stables. The rent was £20 a year. After Mr Cornell, came Sarah Punt, the Punt family ran the inn until the beginning of the twentieth century.

The Chequers

The attractive Chequers is situated at the bottom of Billericay High Street. Billericay is steeped in history, with many ancient buildings. Its most important claim to fame is the fact that Billericay miller, Christopher Martin was one of the three men who chartered the Mayflower, the small ship that took the Pilgrim Fathers to start their new life in America in 1620.

The Chequers is a sixteenth century building once part of the old Chantry farm. The building has been much altered and renovated over the years.

It is first mentioned as an inn in 1765 when Sarah Peacock was the licensee. In the early days most inns had no bars or dining room. Rich customers had private rooms. Food and drink was served to them there. The more humble patrons had to make do with gathering in the kitchen.

In 1874 Samuel John Heard lived there with his wife and eight children, three lodgers and one domestic servant. To make ends meet, with all those mouths to feed Samuel was also a carpenter and undertaker. His wife made straw hats in the little time she had spare. One of their sons became a local carrier, the other son worked on the P&O liners as a butcher. Later he opened his own business at Orsett and another at Vange. Behind the Chequers was the ancient Chantry Barn, a thatched building built of half tree trunks.

BLACKMORE

The Bull.

In 1615 Blackmore had five inns, The Barge, The Black Bull, The Leather Bottle, The Prince Albert and The Bull. Now the Barge and Black Bull are no more.

The famous Essex historian Morant tells that in Blackmore, near the church there was once a Priory. There workmen found a leaden coffin a yard long filled with bones.

Legend has it that when Henry VIII *' had a mind to be lost in the embraces of his courtesans.'* he would visit Blackmore and stop at The Bull on his way to one of his 'houses of pleasure' The house in question was named Jericho. When asked about Henry's whereabouts his courtiers would say,

"He has gone to Jericho"

The story goes that Henry set up his mistress in one of the nearby cottages and there she brought up his illegitimate son.

The Bull with its low, beamed ceilings and huge red brick fireplace has been changed over the years. At one end is a room called the cycle shop where bicycle memorabilia is displayed. This room was certainly a shop, at one time it was a cobbler or boot repairer's. Later it became a haberdasher's shop.

BRAINTREE

The White Hart

The White Hart is situated at the junction of the Bocking and Coggeshall roads. There is reputed to have been an inn there since Roman times. The present day White Hart probably started life in the mid-fourteenth century as a grand manor house for some important merchant or farmer. It has certainly been an inn since the late sixteenth century, when it was owned by John Pavyet. In common with most ancient inns the White Hart was used for all kinds of village activities. It was the meeting place for various organisations, a court room, where one unfortunate man was fined ten shillings for non-attendance at church on ten occasions. Soldiers were billeted there, deserters were court martialled there. Later it became a lecture room, meeting place for the Masonic lodge and many other organisations and societies. The elegant Assembly Room on the first floor was the venue for many a grand ball, dinner or concert.

From 1744 the White Hart was one of the important coaching and posting inns. Letters were carried by post boys. They dashed through the countryside at speeds of around five miles an hour, stopping at post houses for light refreshments and to change horses. Coaches also stopped there to change horses and to drop off, or take on, passengers on the journey from London to Suffolk and Norfolk. The journey from London to Braintree took seven hours.

By 1820 roads and coaches had been improved, the journey took just five hours and cost eight shillings for a seat inside and five shillings outside.

During the nineteenth century coaching inns became more and more prosperous. They began to employ staff. Porters and bootblacks took care of the passengers, while ostlers and stable boys looked after the horses. At one time the White Hart Tap next door was run by the local farrier, who was able to attend to the hundreds of horses that put up there.

Around the middle of the nineteenth century the local doctor, a great character and practical joker was a regular attender at the White Hart. There are many stories of his exploits. One night the local builder, also a frequent visitor to the pub stayed too long and drank too much and was quite incapable of taking himself home at closing time. The doctor brought the builder's horse and trap round to the front door of the inn. The builder was also the local undertaker and by chance there was a coffin in the back of the cart. The doctor and his friends loaded the unfortunate builder into the coffin and sent the horse on its way. Quite a shock for the builder's family when the horse finally found its way home.

In 1941 a high explosive bomb fell on Braintree destroying the shops opposite the White Hart whose ancient timbers hardly suffered any damage. Not like the accident in 1682 when the floor of a room full of people collapsed. Fortunately the only injury then was a broken leg.

The local hunt met at the White Hart, as did the annual May Fair. At the Fair in 1905 Charles Thurston delighted the crowds with his wonderful bioscope. Each evening he would show silent films and play popular tunes on the musical organ.

For many years an egg and poultry market was held every Wednesday in the stable yard of the White Hart. This was closed down as recently as the mid 1960s.

BULPHAN

The Old Plough House

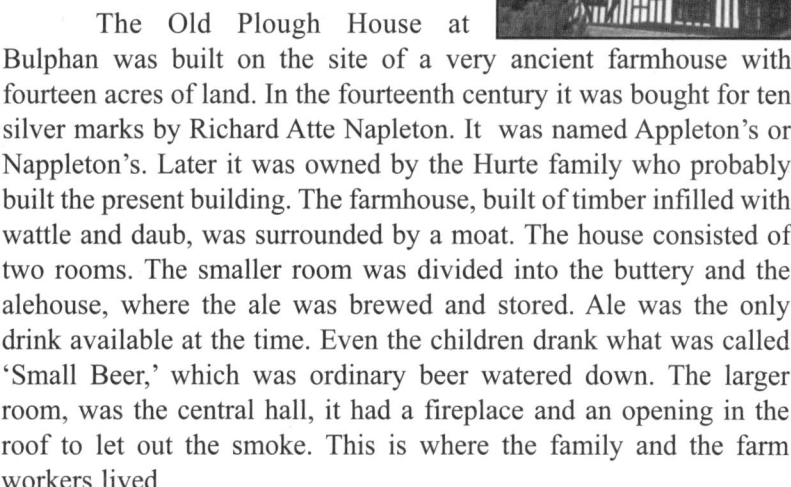

The Old Plough House at Bulphan was built on the site of a very ancient farmhouse with fourteen acres of land. In the fourteenth century it was bought for ten silver marks by Richard Atte Napleton. It was named Appleton's or Nappleton's. Later it was owned by the Hurte family who probably built the present building. The farmhouse, built of timber infilled with wattle and daub, was surrounded by a moat. The house consisted of two rooms. The smaller room was divided into the buttery and the alehouse, where the ale was brewed and stored. Ale was the only drink available at the time. Even the children drank what was called 'Small Beer,' which was ordinary beer watered down. The larger room, was the central hall, it had a fireplace and an opening in the roof to let out the smoke. This is where the family and the farm workers lived

The Hurte family owned the farm for the best part of two hundred years. When Henry Hurte died, in the early sixteenth century, he bequeathed part of his money to local churches and the rest to make sure that his sons were well educated and brought up as good honest God-fearing citizens. Some of the family seem to have let him down. John Hurte was accused of assaulting and beating Robert Cock so badly that he *'despaired of his life.'* Another of the family was charged with profaning God on the Sabbath.

In the seventeenth century a first floor was built, at first it was used to store grain, later as bedrooms. The chimney records the date as 1632 and is thought to be the time that the minstrel gallery was demolished and the fireplace and chimney built.

Appleton's Farm saw many changes and went through hard times as well as prosperous times. After the Hurte family left there were several owners. Eventually the farm and its ninety five acres were sold for £650. The land was divided and the farm was sold in 1897.

It wasn't until the twentieth century that it became an inn.

CANEWDON

The Anchor

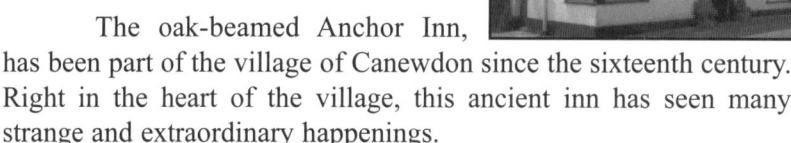

The oak-beamed Anchor Inn, has been part of the village of Canewdon since the sixteenth century. Right in the heart of the village, this ancient inn has seen many strange and extraordinary happenings.

Canewdon has always been closely associated with witches. Superstition says that while the nearby church tower stands there will always be six witches in Canewdon. One of the greatest Essex wizards lived in a tiny cottage near the Anchor. Tall thin and unkempt with piercing eyes, he was master of the witches. He would call them up and will them to dance in the churchyard. The locals would peep through the window of his scruffy cottage and see him dancing with his familiars, even the tables and chairs joined in the dancing .

The church tower is a landmark that can be seen for miles, indeed, locals used to say that from the top of the tower you can see seven hundred churches. In fact you could see seven (Rochford) hundred churches. There are five bells in the tower. When the fifth bell, made in London by Thomas Mears in 1791, was ready to be suspended in the tower, the locals turned it upside down outside the Anchor Inn and filled it with beer. A merry time was had by all. Bells used to be baptised, given a name and solemnly dedicated. It was said that the people of Canewdon could think of nothing more appropriate for their new bell than this *'heathenish baptism and copious drinking of beer.'*

It has always been thought that the Anchor was the home of Sarah, a witch burned at the stake during the great seventeenth century witch hunt. She still lives at the inn in spirit. Many strange happenings have been reported by various landlords, some people have even seen a ghostly figure in the old disused cellar. A witches or devil's circle was found on the floor of one of the bedrooms. There is a secret room upstairs and a trap door in the chimney thought to be a priest hole. Seven dusty figures of witches hang by the bar. It is supposed to be unlucky to touch them even for cleaning. The ghost still make itself felt at times. Objects are moved or broken, inexplicable noises are heard. In recent years, mediums have revealed that the ghost is not named Sarah, but Kathleen Spurrier, who was found guilty of being a witch and burned near the church in 1666.

The Chequers

A little further along the main street towards the ancient church is the Chequers Inn.

The inn sign the 'Chequers' is a very ancient sign. Examples have been found at Pompeii. The sign was brought here by the Romans. It usually depicted a chequered board, announcing that a game similar to draughts was played there. Later it became a sign that money could be exchanged there. Some 'Chequers' are named after the chequer or wild service tree which had a strange chequered patterned bark. Its berries were used in the brewing of beer.

The more modern sign shows a picture of Chequers, the home of the Prime Minister, which was given to the nation by Viscount Lee and is the Official Residence of the Prime Minister.

The Chequers at Canewdon has been altered and modernised several times. The beer cellar has been turned into a children's room. At the beginning of the twentieth century the Chequers was a popular meeting place for cyclists. They would stop there for afternoon tea, or to find lodgings for the night.

CANVEY ISLAND

The King Canute

The property known as the Red Cow was owned by Thomas Worrin Blythe of Stanford le Hope. When he died the Stanford le Hope Brewery, the Rising Sun beerhouse at Stanford le Hope, the Red Cow beerhouse and the adjoining land at Canvey Island were sold to Messrs Westwood Squier, Joseph Squier and Frank Mercer, all of Horndon-on-the-Hill, brewers and maltsters, for the sum of six thousand pounds. This was in 1902.

The Olde Red Cow was a favourite meeting place for the villagers. Next to the inn stood the blacksmith's forge. Opposite the pub was the village pump, the main water supply for the village. A huge crowd gathered to watch when the first bucket of water was drawn from the pump in 1889. A horse trough was also erected there for the animals. The Red Cow was used as a courthouse by the coroner. He went by pony and trap across to the island from the mainland. The doctor also visited the islanders on horseback. His surgery was in South Benfleet. Canvey had no doctor of its own until 1911 when the Canvey Medical Association was formed. Visitors to the pub were served Thurrocks Ales. It was owned by the Seabrook Breweries.

In 1953 when the East Coast suffered the terrible floods, Canvey Island was very badly affected. Most of the Island was flooded. The townspeople had to leave their homes and take shelter in halls and schools in Benfleet. Being on slightly higher ground than most of the island, the Red Cow was more or less left high and dry and was chosen as the headquarters for the rescue operations. The rescue mission was named King Canute, after King Canute who tried to stop the tide. It was to the Red Cow that the survivors were taken before leaving the island and it was here on the forecourt that 500,000 sandbags were filled, ready to be used to try and stem the flood. Fifty-eight Canvey people died in the flood. The Queen Mother and Princess Margaret visited survivors in the Benfleet school where they were being looked after.

After the floods, the Red Cow was renamed the King Canute. A plaque was placed in the bar stating:-

This Hostelry then known as the Red Cow was used as headquarters by those engaged in the epic defence and rebuilding of the sea wall breached by floods Febuary 1953. At this very point the waters ebbed and hence it was renamed The King Canute.

The Lobster Smack

The Lobster Smack's remote location amongst the marshes made it the ideal place for all kinds of illegal goings on, smuggling being one of the most popular. It was easy to sail up the creeks and unload the goods at the inn which was almost on the sea wall. However it was fatal to leave the goods in one place for too long, so they were often transferred to the Church, another favourite hiding place for the ill-gotten gains.

One story tells of how revenue men were on the prowl and the farmer smuggler was anxious to collect goods from his hiding place in the church, but the priest was holding a service. After a great deal of thought the farmer rushed into the church and begged the priest to go to his house which he said was being haunted. He implored the priest to exorcise the evil spirits. The priest and all the congregation, hurried off to the farmer's home and carried out the service of exorcism. Meanwhile the farmer and his friends got to work and quickly transferred the goods to another hide-out and removed all traces of their illegal smuggling activities.

Another popular and illegal activity that went on at the Lobster Smack was bare knuckle fighting. Fights took place on the marshes, where it was easy to spot anyone approaching. The inn was used for changing rooms and refreshments. These knuckle fights were famous throughout the county. One fight between Aaron Jones and Tom Sawyer lasted over two hours. After sixty-five rounds it became too dark to see what was happening, so the referee had to call a draw.

Dutch eel boats arriving in the Thames estuary anchored at the island and crews rowed ashore to the Lobster Smack before making their way to Billingsgate Fish Market to unload their catch.

In Great Expectations, Dickens mentions the Lobster Smack. He hired a steamer from London to Southend to gain background for the book. At the end of the story he describes the desolate mud flats, river and the pub, where Herbert Starr, Provis and Pip spent the night, as a *'dirty place enough,'* where they were given eggs and bacon.

One night in 1933 fire broke out at the Lobster Smack. Luckily one of the guests, Dr. Porter awoke and realised the place was on fire. He woke the landlord, who sent his son to call the telegraph operator and tell her to call the police and fire brigade. A maroon was fired. Firemen left their beds and dashed to the fire station in nearby Benfleet. When they arrived at the Lobster Smack, the firefighters managed to put out the fire which had taken such a hold that they had to rip out the fireplaces and tear up the floorboards. Finally the building was declared safe. That the Lobster Smack remains standing is due entirely to the Benfleet fire brigade. *"They saved us from danger and the old inn for future generations of Essex folk to visit "* said Mr Whent the landlord.

During the second World War the Lobster Smack became part of the Royal Navy, it was used as a River Emergency shore station. There were many of these along the river from the estuary to Tower Pier. The upstairs of the pub became the sleeping accommodation for the men and the tap room became the mess. A hand-operated lift connected the two.

In 1944 two American B17 aircraft known as 'flying fortresses' were flying over Canvey in formation with thirty other planes, some damaged, some having only three engines. One aircraft suddenly plummeted colliding with another named Heavenly Body II, flown by 2nd Lieut. Fred Kauffman. Some of the crew managed to bale out and were taken to the Lobster Smack after being rescued from the river. The other aircraft, flying over Canvey avoided the populated Island, tried to land on the mud flats but crashed and burst into flames. The plane, piloted by Lieut. Ramacitti crashed into the Thames Estuary, off Canvey Point. Over fifty years later a plaque to the memory of the crews was placed at the Paddocks Community Centre.

CLACTON

The Queen's Head.

The elegant Queen's Head at Great Clacton has been an inn for over three hundred years. Originally the building was a private house named the Layes. By the late 1600's it was known as the Queen's Head.

During the Napoleonic wars when the military were stationed in Clacton, the Queen's head became the town's principal meeting place. The landlord had the inn enlarged and added the big elegant bow window. At the back there was a brewery and maltings. The room upstairs was used as a ballroom. The local farmers used it for their weekly corn market. On the great table in the centre of the room would be a collection of clay pipes and tins of tobacco, for the use of anyone who wished to help themselves. Anyone failing to close the lid of the tin was fined sixpence. These meeting would go on into the night and often into the next day. The church vestry meeting also took place at the Queen's Head and also their Easter Dinner which started in the afternoon and carried on all night and into the following day. These dinners went on annually until the beginning of the First World War.

In 1844 the brewer John Cobbold bought the inn and the adjoining blacksmith's shop for £1,550.

The Ship.

The Ship Inn at great Clacton was once part of an estate named Stringers. Its owner Walter Stringer was horribly murdered by one of his neighbours. Later it came into the possession of Philip Gardiner a wealthy London apothecary. In 1709 it was sold by his daughter for £45. The sale included an orchard and one acre of land. It was bought by Thomas Joy who turned it into an inn and named it The Ship, possibly because its long timber frame resembled the hull of a ship. The Ship was one of the main meeting places is the village. The court was held there and parish meetings, auctions, and many village get togethers and entertainments. The village fair always took place on the green in front of the Inn. Joy put in a bowling green, a very popular pastime with the villagers. When war against the French was declared the locals assembled at the Ship and marched through the village pledging allegiance to the King. When an enemy ship foundered off the shore and some of the French crew made their getaway in the town, they were quickly captured by the locals, who later met at The Ship to celebrate by drinking a hogshead (almost four hundred pints) of beer. The Ship remained in the hands of the Joy family for over a hundred years. It was finally bought by John Cobbold for £700.

As Clacton became more popular as a seaside resort, the landlords of the local inns encouraged visitors to spend their money by holding various functions and competitions and supplying them with the much needed refreshments. A landlord of The Ship set up a bathing machine on the seafront. Until the beginning of the 20th century, one end of The Ship was a shop and the other end a schoolroom.

COGGESHALL

Woolpack

The Woolpack was built around the beginning of the fifteenth century and is thought to have been a hostelry for wool merchants. Parts of it are considered to be of an earlier date, as the north wing is out of line with the rest of the building. There is a theory that it was built on the site of a Roman Villa., Roman tiles have been found there.

In 1665 it was bought by the Reverend Thomas Lowrey. He had been ejected from ministry of the Church of England after the reformation. It was his private house and not a rectory, although he used it as a chapel for non-conformists. He was a great friend of Thomas Paycocke, a well known wool merchant who lived in the famous Paycocke House which is now owned by the National Trust. When Lowrey died, in 1690 the house went to his son Jeremy along with £900. His daughter was left various pieces of silver. £5 went to eight non-conformist ministers. Jeremy in turn left the property to his son Jeremiah· who was an apothecary in London. He sold the property, which had been converted into an hostelry, to George Long.

The name Woolpack is thought to have been chosen as being appropriate at the time when many of the Protestant weavers who were fleeing from Catholic persecution made their homes in Coggeshall which became the centre of the wool trade. The name of the inn was changed for a short time to the Woolpack and Punchbowl. The Woolpack was a meeting place for the locals and the centre of village festivities. In 1678 Abraham Emmings roasted a whole bullock there at the Shrove Tuesday party. There is a record of soldiers setting up a maypole outside the door at the Mayday celebrations in 1693.

The Woolpack was sold at auction in September 1828, when

the brewers who owned it and other inns in the area were declared bankrupt. The freehold house is described as being in a desirable part of Church Street on the Halstead and Colne Road. Having numerous rooms, stable for eight horses, with loft over. Pigeons and a piece of ground 14ft by 20ft at the east side of the passage. It was well supplied with water, and in the occupation of Sarah Buck.

The exterior was altered in the nineteenth century. The beams were covered up, then later the plaster was removed, the beams exposed and fresh plaster put between the beams. In 1932 the brewers removed this plaster and brought the exterior back to its original state. An inner wall was removed and a magnificent fireplace was revealed. A cash book was found dated 1820, this showed that the inn was also used as a shop. This ancient inn with its beams, low ceilings, and great character is now a Grade I listed building.

COLCHESTER

The George

The medieval George was probably an inn as long ago as the fifteenth century when it was named the George and Dragon. The cellars were dated at around the middle of the fifteenth century. The building was altered and enlarged at the beginning of the seventeenth century.

At one time the ostler, John Lyon was keen on a young lady who worked in the tailor's shop next door. But Frances had a fancy for her employer. When confronted with this by her swain she denied having any feelings for the tailor. John refused to believe her and said he would leave her if she would not wish her one eye would fall into his outheld cap. Frances had lost one eye during an attack of smallpox and was reluctant to risk losing the other one, so she refused to wish. True to his word John left her. He never found another love except money, which he hoarded relentlessly. He died quite a rich man in 1800 aged sixty-four. He left his money to various good causes including the Methodist run charity school and five pounds to provide loaves for the inmates of the alms houses.

The George is known for the small part it played at the time of the Red Barn Murder. Maria Martin was murdered by her lover and buried in the Red Barn. Her murderer was named Corder. After he had been charged, he was taken to the George where he stayed the night, handcuffed to the bed by one hand and to a police constable by the other, this was in 1828.

Like many important inns the George was once a coaching inn. At the side of the building is evidence of the archway where the coaches drove into the courtyard. There is also evidence of two little medieval shop windows.

The Hole in the Wall

Standing on the old Roman wall is the Hole in the Wall. The present building is not ancient but is on the site of Colchester's earliest inn. During renovations, a number of Roman artefacts were discovered. The inn was called Woodcocks at one time and was the meeting place of the Royalist officers. There is a story that a secret tunnel was dug underneath the inn as an escape route from Cromwell's soldiers. After the siege of Colchester the Roundheads changed the name from Woodcocks to The King's Head, this was to celebrate the fact that King Charles the First had been beheaded.

When the railway came to the town. The inn was extended, and several extra rooms were built. The hole was made to give a better view of the new Railway station. Cab drivers were able to sit in the pub and see the station through the hole. When they saw the train approaching, they would down their drink and drive round to the station to collect their passengers. The locals nicknamed it the Hole in the Wall and the name has been adopted by popular consent.

The Marquis of Granby

The Marquis of Granby, or as it has recently been renamed, Ye Old Marquis, dates back to 1500, when it was the home of a rich, important man. A lovely inn covered with brilliant hanging baskets on the outside, full of character inside, with great ancient beams, wonderful, strange and bizarre carvings. Some of the magnificent features are thought to be the finest examples of Tudor architecture and carvings in the county.

This impressive inn, standing on North Hill, is thought to have once been the home of the Keeper of the North Gate. It was named after John Manners, Marquess of Granby, eldest son of the Duke of Rutland. In 1741 he was Member of Parliament for Grantham. The saying 'to go into something bald headed' is said to have come about by the fact that at a time when it was the fashion to wear a wig, the Marquess, although he was completely bald, refused to wear a wig. A brilliant soldier, a generous and popular leader, brave to a fault, he was appointed Commander-in-chief of the British Army during the Seven Years War. When the war ended he set up many of his officers as innkeepers. They in gratitude named the hostelries after their benefactor.

A newspaper article from the mid 1800's tells a strange tale of the naked body of a young woman found in an outhouse. At the inquest, which was held at the Marquess of Granby the verdict was that she had died from 'a visitation of God.'

DUNMOW

The Flitch of Bacon,

An inn has stood on this site for nearly 400 years. It is thought to be the only British pub with this name. It is named after the ancient custom of the Dunmow Flitch, which originated in Little Dunmow at the time of Henry III. Robert Fitzwalter instituted the custom, which declared that any man who had not regretted his marriage 'sleeping or waking' for a year and a day was invited to go to Dunmow and claim the gammon of bacon. The applicant, watched by the Prior and all the villagers, had to kneel on two sharp stones and swear an oath. Then he was carried on the 'flitch chair' around the village.

Some of the records of early Flitch winners are in the British museum. Richard Wright won the bacon in 1445 and Stephen Samuel 1467. Chaucer mentioned the ancient custom,

'The bacon was not fet for him I trowe
That some men han in Essex at Dunmowe.'

On the outside wall of the Inn is a wooden plaque stating:-

Painted in Gold ye Flitch behold
Of famed Dunmow ye Boaste
Then here should I call fond Couples all
And Pledge it in a Toaste

The inn sign is a gold painted side of bacon.

More recently the flitch of bacon was provided by the nearby Flitch Bacon Company which opened in 1909, at the same time as two breweries were opened in the same area near the station. The bacon company changed hands several times and sadly closed down in 1984.

The Saracen's Head

The sign outside depicts the head of a fierce looking, sword brandishing, nomad of the Syrian or Arabian desert at the time of the Roman Empire. The inn itself has a fairly modern exterior but it is much older than it looks, possibly Tudor. One landlord was the father of Richard Deane who was Lord Mayor of London in 1628. Oliver Cromwell is said to have stayed at the inn. Another landlord, a charming and popular man was caught trying to rob the carriage of one of his rich guests. It turned out he was a well known highwayman and smuggler.

At one time the village pump stood outside the Saracen's head but the increasing traffic made it a hazard and the authorities decided to re-site it. Locals were not best pleased with this. They wanted their pump to remain where it had always been. Some blamed the landlord of the Saracen's Head. He was a foreigner from Felstead and therefore not really to be trusted. They said he had diverted the water to his own yard. There were fights and disputes.but the authorities were determined that the pump would be moved. The locals were determined it would stay put. The authorities filled up the well and locals came in the night, took out all the stones and had a new pump made by the local blacksmith. When officials and the local constable started to remove the new pump the locals were furious. Fights broke out, sticks and stones were thrown. Eventually the Magistrate's clerk read the Riot Act. Several of the men were arrested and charged with various offences including breaking the windows of the Saracen's Head, refusing to obey the Magistrate and failing to keep the peace.

Two men were sentenced to two years and others to six months in Chelmsford prison.

FAMBRIDGE

The Ferry Boat Inn

The Inn dates back to the 15th century. It started out as a row of three cottages built for the use of farm workers. Like many ancient buildings the Ferry Boat has very low ceilings and flimsy foundations, mainly bits of wood, plaster and reeds. The Inn was at one time right on the riverbank, it was possible to row up to the bar, but the changing riverbed and sea defences have altered the coast line and it is no longer quite so near the river. Outside is part of a small wall, all that is left of what was once the only defence against the tide. Flooding was a constant hazard. The river is still just a stone's throw away. There was a ferry far back in 1579.

A Mr Richeman was accused of obstructing the way to the ferry. Later the boats were found to be too dangerous for passengers to use and in 1625 the ferryman increased the charge for foot passengers to two pence. The ferry took passengers across the River Crouch to South Fambridge. At the end of the 19th century William Palmer was the victualler and ferryman, a job he shared with his son. He lived at the Ferry Boat Inn with his wife, son, daughter and two labourer lodgers. The ferry ceased ferrying in the 70's. The ferryman at the time was Reg Watson, a regular at the pub. A plaque to him is on his favourite spot at the bar. Two mischievous ghosts haunt the Ferry Boat, they are forever dropping and moving things around. One ghost is thought to be an old ferryman.

The pub is friendly and full of interest. A collection of sailor's hats with names of ships from all parts of the globe are fixed to the ceiling. Pinned at the back of the bar are banknotes from all over the world. Also displayed with pride are boxing gloves. One pair that belonged to Mohamed Ali and another was once used by Frank Bruno.

The Anchor.

In 1556 two properties named The Ferry-lands and Betts, belonged to the Harry family. These properties changed hands several times. With Ferry-lands came the rights of toll across the ferry. This right was shared equally with the farm on the north bank of the river. It was here at Ferry-lands that Captain Thomas Cammock and Frances, daughter of Lord Rich, Earl of Warwick made their daring escape.

Cammock was travelling as escort with the Earl from Lees Priory to Rochford Hall. Captain Cammock and Frances were in love but the Earl would not have approved of their marriage so they decided to elope. They galloped off on Cammock's horse. When they reached the river at South Fambridge to their dismay they found the boat was on the far side. Knowing they were being pursued Captain Cammock decided that he must swim across the river. The water was rough and dangerous. He told Frances she must stay where she was, no harm would come to her. Frances, was adamant *"I will live and die with you"* she said.

They rode their horse into the raging river. Halfway across they saw their pursuers. Their horse, hearing the other beasts began to turn and swim back. With great difficulty they managed to persuade the horse to carry on. At last they reached the North bank and rode on to Maldon. Here they were married. The Earl forgave them. He realised how much she loved him if she was willing to risk her life to be with him.

Thomas, his first wife and Frances his second wife were buried in All Saint's Church Maldon. In the church is also the Cammock Monument placed there in 1602 as a memorial to Thomas, his two wives and their twenty-two children.

It was at the Ferry that a couple from Stambridge Road were 'swum' in the river. Boatmen sailing their corn hoys up to London said they had seen the woman floating on the rough waves. Neighbours complained that she was frequently tending her garden and taking juice from the large headed poppies. This juice was to feed her imps every full moon. The couple named Hart were taken to the river, where a great crowd had gathered to watch. The husband was found to be innocent when he nearly drowned. The wife was tied to a boat by a line, she floated like a cork and was therefore deemed to be a witch. One waterman said he had seen her swimming in the river in a bowl and had been put under a spell by her. When her death bell tolled he found the spell had left him.

The Anchor replaced the Ferry Boat. A very large pub, it was built to serve the workers from the new factory which was opened at Fambridge. The factory made cranes. Sadly this project failed and the factory became derelict. It was later bought by Noel Billing a pioneer aviator. During experiments one of the workman lost his life trying to get a water-plane off the ground. Later the building was used for storage. It seemed to be a doomed building for it was finally destroyed by fire in 1964. Although the hoped for customers from the factory failed to materialise The Anchor is still busy. It is popular with locals and with the many sailing enthusiasts in the area.

FOBBING

The White Lion

The little community of Fobbing is best known for its part in the Peasants Revolt in 1381. The uprising was sparked off by high taxation and low wages. The government introduced the poll tax, which taxed every poll or head in the land. The government also made it illegal for labourers to ask for more wages or to try and find work in another place. This and the poll tax levied on anyone over fifteen, started the revolt. Incited by the local excommunicated priest John Ball, and led by Wat Tyler of Kent and Fobbing's Jack Straw, the enraged peasants charged through the country into London. They released the prisoners from Fleet jail, tore down anything they could lay their hands on. Finally they killed and beheaded the unpopular Archbishop of Canterbury and other victims.

Eventually the young king, Richard promised to grant their requests. Parliament overruled this. The uprising began again. Tens of thousands of labourers were killed, including Wat Tyler and Thomas Baker also of Fobbing. Their heads were placed on pikes over the entrance gate to London Bridge.

All this was many years before the White Lion was built, though its recorded history goes back well over four hundred years. Originally the building was an Essex yeoman's house. A yeoman is a person possessing land valued at an annual value of forty shillings. It was registered as an alehouse in 1767. The licensee was Leonard Rust. Members of the Rust family held the licence for many years. A local lad named Labor was courting the landlord's daughter Elizabeth Rust, but when newcomer William Bogue arrived on the scene the trouble began. William also took a fancy to Elizabeth. Eventually Elizabeth chose William and they were married at the parish church and afterwards made merry at the White Lion. The jilted Labor arrived at the wedding ceremony and the party afterwards. Labor and the groom exchanged a few harsh words, and a few well aimed punches. In the end Brogue and his friends held Labor over the fireplace for a good roasting. Brogue was fined a shilling for punching Labor on the nose.

In 1900 several alterations were made to the premises. In the cellar a note was found it said:

"This partition was put up by William Rust, tenant of the house under Mr Ed Ind brewer of Romford 1823. At the same time he carried on business of general shopkeeper carpenter and undertaker on those premises. Please excuse the spelling as I am in haste Sarah."

In a little prayer book belonging to Elizabeth Rust she has written the names Neptune, Bodsey, Sophia, Avis. These were names of some of the barges based in Fobbing creek. Many barges visited the port and on Oak Apple day on May the 29th the inn would be decorated with flowers and branches. The locals and the bargemen would dance and drink outside the White Lion all day and far into the night. This festival is supposed to have been started by the Reverend John Pell, rector of Fobbing. It has taken place from the time when King Charles II re-established the Church of England calendar and the festivals which had been abolished by Oliver Cromwell.

In the mid 1800s the inn was used by the village as a meeting place for the locals and different clubs, as well as for travellers. There were six bedrooms, nine bedsteads and ten flock beds, two parlours, stables, a chain house and paint house and kitchen. The wine stock was valued at little over eleven pounds with forty pieces of glass and all the mugs. There were also six sailing barges in decent repair, these were valued at £1,253.

FOULNESS

The George & Dragon.

Built about 1650 the George & Dragon was originally three weather boarded cottages but has since undergone many changes. Until the nineteenth century, the island, because of its remote location was the refuge of many a criminal and wanted man. It was also the ideal spot for all kinds of illegal pursuits, dog fighting, smuggling and even deliberate shipwrecking. One of the most popular diversions in the 1800s was bare fist fighting. Fights took place outside the George & Dragon. The most famous fighter in the area was John Bennewith, whose mother was the licensee. Bennewith 'The Foulness Champion' had amongst his opponents The Giant, The Infant and Bullock Bones. As many as two thousand people were known to have turned out to watch him fight.

One of the many Essex witches having had words with one of the farmers put a curse on the island. The curse was a plague of mice. Foulness is a fertile place very suited to farming. Curiously, in the mid seventeenth century the farmers did suffer a great plague of mice. They nested among the molehills eating the grass down to the roots. They were highly infectious to cattle. Suddenly a number of owls appeared over the island and completely wiped them out.

In the 1920's, a bar meal at the George & Dragon consisted of an arrowroot biscuit and a pint of ale. Now visitors to the annual Town Show can expect a far more satisfying fare. At one of the Foulness Show days in the 1930s the bar was packed with people, One of the visitors complained that there were not enough seats Harry Guiver the licensee replied,

"Enough seats, too many backsides".

The Islanders are not overfond of outsiders swarming over their territory. However the annual fete is still a great attraction and takes place every July.

The Island has a very varied history, in 1930 the War Department restricted entry to the general public. In 1953 the Island was very badly flooded.

The Kings Head and the Old Rochford Volunteer have now become obsolete, leaving the George & Dragon as not only the last pub left on the island, but the village shop and post office as well.

FRINTON-ON-SEA

Lock & Barrel

Frinton was designed in Victorian times by Richard Cooper. He wanted his town to be unique. He did not plan for any thing so outlandish as a public house. He wanted the town to be select, and select it remained until September 2000, when its very first pub was opened and Frinton could no longer boast that it was the only pub free town in England. Eight years previously, after a great deal of public opposition, Frinton's first fish and chip shop was opened.

It was Eamonn Ryan, rich entrepreneur, who put the cat among the pigeons and proposed opening a pub in this quiet, genteel little community, where no coaches are allowed in the town and dogs are banned from the beaches and no games are allowed on the greensward. The locals opposed him and the battle raged for over three years. Mr Ryan was determined that he was going to open a pub in Frinton, even if he had to run it himself. The residents were just as determined not to allow it. A hundred and seventy people wrote to complain, over a thousand opposed the plan. Not that they are snobs. They just don't want anything to change. Finally the council agreed. The pub was given the green light.

Shepherd Neame the Brewers who manage the pub, sell a beer named Spitfire. They cleverly organised a flypast by a Spitfire aircraft at the first opening time. Crowds of people flocked to the High Street to witness the opening. The elegant pub was packed. According to the secretary of the Residents Association, the arrival of the pub marked 'the worst day in Frinton since the Luftwaffe beat up the town in 1944.' A remark that has found its way into the Times Book of Quotations. Mr Ryan assured residents that the opening of the Lock and Barrel would not mean the end of civilisation in Frinton. The pub will always have a strict dress code and will not allow drinking from bottles.

The building was originally the long established ironmonger's shop Blowers and Cooper which had been a feature of the town since 1912. It was opened by two friends, Thomas Blower and George Cooper, both from Diss in Norfolk.

A competition was organised to find an original name for the first pub 'through the gate' of Frinton. The Lock & Barrel was chosen as a reminder of the kind of hardware once sold from the original shop on the site.

GREAT LEIGHS

Ye Old Anne's Castle.

Ye Old St Anne's Castle at Great Leighs claims the distinction of being the country's oldest inn. It was first mentioned in 1171. It is said that it was once a hermitage. Pilgrims passing by on their way to Canterbury to the shrine of Thomas a Becket who was canonised in 1173 often stopped there for rest and refreshment. Eventually it became a popular place to stay on the long journey. During the reformation the hermitage was seized and turned into an inn.

There have been several ghosts haunting the inn. One of the bedrooms was haunted by the Witch of Leighs who was burned at the stake. She terrorised the landlords and locals for years, until bulldozers uncovered what was thought to be her grave. Charred bones and funeral pyre were buried under a boulder nearby. Once the remains were properly buried no more was heard from her.

Inns, being the main meeting place for the locals, the landlord was often called upon to take part in all manner of events.

One night, the churchwarden discovered the naked body of a woman lying on the ground by the churchyard. He hurried to St Anne's Castle, woke the landlord and asked him to come and see what was occurring. Nearby, they found a horse and cart, a shovel and some pistols. In the cart was a box about the size and shape of a coffin. The horse and cart were traced to their owner, Samuel Clarke. He was charged with taking away a body and sentenced at Chelmsford Assizes to three months. The dead woman, Joanna Chinnerey, had been recently buried wearing her favourite dress. Clarke was also found guilty of stealing her clothes. For that offence he was transported for seven years.

HARWICH

The Three Cups.

The Three Cups at Harwich has been licensed as an inn for over four hundred years. It was built in Tudor times. The name is said to come from the coat of arms of the Salter's Company. There is a more romantic story attached to the name.

The nearby church is dedicated to Saint Nicholas, patron saint of sailors. The story tells of three young girls who were desperately poor and could think of no way out of their poverty but by selling themselves. Nicholas discovered their plight and to save them from prostitution threw three bags of gold into their room one night. The three bags of gold, tied up at the top are supposed to look like three inverted goblets and so the nearby inn was named The Three Cups and the inn sign showed three golden goblets.

Many famous people have visited The Three Cups, including Frederick the Great, Louis XVIII, Nelson, who addressed the crowd from the balcony. Lady Hamilton, in fact she is still there, her ghost so they say, still haunts the inn. Sir Francis Drake and the Lord High Admiral were Harwich men. They met at The Three Cups after the defeat of the Armada.. George II drank there incognito before taking the coach to his home. In 1821 the body of Queen Caroline of Brunswick rested there on its way to Germany to be buried. Queen Elizabeth I is said to have stayed there and to have very much enjoyed her stay. The famous Mayflower was a Harwich ship. Her captain, Christopher Jones was a Harwich man.

In 1753 The Three Cups was run by Mr Hallsted. An enterprising kind of man Mr Hallsted opened a bath house, near Angel Gate. The next year Thomas Cobbold set up a rival bath house known as Brewers Baths. Mr Cobbold became so rich through this enterprise he bought the Three Cups and most of the inns in the area.

The Three Cups was the meeting place for many civic functions. Lavish Assembly balls took place there. During the Elections in the 19th century The Three Cups was headquarters for the parliamentary candidates as there was no other place fit for a gentleman to stay. The locals discovered that at the inn they could sell their vote to the highest bidder. A great deal of money changed hands, and the proprietor Mr Bull made a small fortune from the vast amount of liquor sold at the time.

Despite this, he still made it clear at the inquiry that was later held into corruption, that he disapproved of the underhand goings on that had taken place.

Many alterations have taken place at The Three Cups. The ancient stud work front with its overhanging upper floor was changed to the Georgian style. Sadly, much later, part of the rear of the inn was demolished including the famous Nelson Room which had been full of Nelson relics. The famous old clematis plant which grew for many years in the courtyard also fell victim to progress.

HEMPSTEAD

The Bluebell.

The notorious highwayman Dick Turpin was born at The Bluebell Inn, Hempstead in 1705. His parents were John and Mary Turpin. It wasn't called The Bluebell then, it was the Crown. Later it was named the Rose and Crown. Dick Turpin has been portrayed as a glamorous and romantic character. In fact, spoilt by his mother and father Dick grew to become a rogue and crook from quite an early age. He went to work as apprentice to a butcher and promptly took to cattle stealing. He also poached deer from Epping forest, these were sent to London where there was a thriving Black Market trade in venison. Next he tried his hand at robbery and smuggling. Then he joined a gang of footpads, highwaymen going about their trade on foot rather than on horseback. He soon became their leader and led them into many villainous exploits around Essex and the outskirts of London. His activities included robbing several of the churches in Chingford and Barking. He and three other villains were caught in a tavern in the city. Dick managed to escape. His three companions were hanged. Dick thought it wise to move out of the area for a time and it was then that he acquired his horse, Black Bess.

Turpin is credited with many daring deeds, one is his famous ride from London to York. He had committed a robbery in London and in order to give himself an alibi, he rode his horse across the river at Gravesend through Billericay, Saffron Walden, Cambridge and on to York. The journey took just fifteen hours which everyone said was an impossibility. This story is often credited to another highwayman Swift Nick Nevenson.

After the demise of his partners, Dick began operating in the Cambridge area and met up with another villain, Tom King. They found a secret hiding place in Epping Forest, known as Turpin's

Cave, here they were joined by another partner. During an attempted rescue of Tom King from the Red Lion in Whitechapel, Dick accidentally shot and killed Tom. He escaped, moved to Yorkshire and set up as a horse dealer using his wife's maiden name, Palmer. Unfortunately for Dick a schoolteacher came by a letter written by Dick Palmer the horse dealer, to his brother at the Rose and Crown. He recognised the handwriting as that of Dick Turpin the horse stealer. Dick went to the gallows in York in 1739.

Opposite The Bluebell is a ring of trees known as 'Turpin's Ring' here Dick played as a child. It is thought to be a cock-fighting pit. There have been alterations to the inn since those times but mementoes of the infamous highwayman, his trial and eventual execution are displayed around the bars. The peephole Dick used to make sure the coast was clear can still bee seen in the ceiling, but it is no longer possible to peep through it, as it has been blocked up.

HOCKLEY

The Bull

The Bull is one of the most ancient inn names. It usually meant that the barbaric practise of bull-baiting took place there. In the middle ages bull baiting was considered to be a fine sport. The bulls would often be bred at, or near the pub and on the day the sport was to take place a bull would be led into the yard and tied to a post. Then when everyone was assembled, the dogs would be let out. The trained terriers would yap and snap at the bull's legs and feet. The unfortunate bull maddened by this would stamp on, toss and trample the dogs. Bets would be placed on which dog could keep up the vicious attack the longest.

At one time there was a Bull Inn in Rayleigh. The animals were bred at the rear of Bull Lane. On the day of the event the beast would be led down Bull Lane and haltered to a ring in a post in the centre of the yard. Locals became angry at this cruel sport taking place at the Bull and they, blaming the landlord decided to take the law into their own hands. Twenty or so men led by the blacksmith broke into the inn and set about the landlord. They were later tried for unlawful assembly and for breaking into the Bull and assaulting the landlord and another man until they *'despaired of their lives.'*

The Bull at Hockley is an attractive building full of character. Until recently a table skittles game was a popular pastime there. One morning in 1940 a maid was dusting in one of the bars when she noticed a piece of paper in the panelling. She was sure it had not been there last time she dusted. When she opened it she found it to be rather scorched and torn but very interesting. It told how in 1804, Dandy Jack one of the last footpads in Essex had hidden his ill-gotten gains behind the fireplace which was then being installed at the rear of the taproom. Then he took himself to the barn and ended his evil ill-spent life *'by the rope, in the old barn in Follie Lane.'* The note says that whether it was true or not he didn't know but *'tis a strange fact'* that the day after Dandy Jack hanged himself the landlord of the Bull was found dead.

After the death of the landlord the inn was empty for many years and was finally taken over by a man named Webster. The writer of the note says he told the new owner the story of the gold, but he being a Londoner *'did but laff it off.'* It is my wish, he continues that on the death of this Webster, my son John do buy the Bull and search for the ... and there the manuscript ends. At the top of the paper was a drawing of Hockley Woods and an arrow pointing to the inn. Another drawing shows the Smithy facing the inn and Folly Lane at the side. When the manuscript was found, the Bull was owned by Mr and Mrs Bowen who had been there for nearly fifty years. Mrs Bowen explained that the Bull was over four hundred years old. She supposed the note had been hidden in the panelling and had gradually worked loose with the vibration of the traffic.

In 1874 Charles Lark was landlord of the Bull in Hockley. He lived there with Sarah his wife, their six children, a servant and two lodgers, who were labourers.

By 1891 the Larks' had taken over the nearby Spa.

The Spa

About 1838, Robert Clay and his wife Letitia, a chronic asthmatic, moved to Hockley. It wasn't long before they noticed Letitia's health and general well-being improved. Her cough had almost gone. They put this down to the local water.

This came to the ears of Mr. Fawcett, a London solicitor. He engaged Richard Phillips to analyse the water. He reported that it contained four ingredients; common salt, bi-carbonate of lime, sulphate of magnesia or Epsom salts and sulphate of lime. There was no iron or anything that can militate against its use for inflammatory complaints.

A Dr Granvill was consulted, he pronounced the waters to be *'efficacious to children suffering from want of ossification of the bones and those who were inclined to have rickety and bandy legs, and for dyspeptic disorders.'* At great expense the pump room was built.

The opening was celebrated with a public breakfast. Dreaming of another Bath or Tunbridge Wells, a great deal of money was spent building an hotel. All seemed to be going well. Vans ran to London with fresh supplies of this water. The Spa was opened. However the public were not impressed. Hockley was declared dull. They refused to patronise the Spa.

Benton in the mid 1800's says: *'the whole has now a dilapidated appearance and the hotel has since been let at £10 per annum as a beer shop and the unfortunate spa room as a Baptist Chapel.'*

The hotel was built on the site of a cottage inhabited by William Hazard who died in 1808 aged 105. His life was probably prolonged by the beneficial water.

One very important local person having been declining in health had a high opinion of the healing properties of the water. He sent his servant at regular intervals for this beverage. After several months his health improved greatly.

Some time later it was discovered that the servant stopped off at the Hawk in Battlesbridge on his way to the Spa and being too lazy to make the journey filled the containers at the nearby pump.

Robert Clay died in 1843 at the age of seventy two, and Letitia died four years later aged sixty eight.

HORNDON-ON-THE-HILL.

The Bell.

The delightful Bell Inn at Horndon-on-the-Hill was built in the early part of the fifteenth century. It was a coaching inn of considerable importance at the time. The old Roman Road went from Chelmsford through Horndon-on-the-Hill, across the Thames, on to Highams Causeway in Kent, then to Dover or Canterbury.

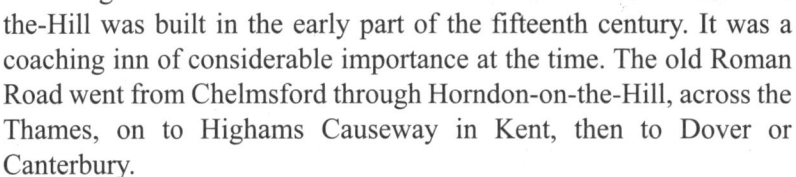

Horndon-on-the-Hill was a very important and wealthy town. Sheep were grazed on the plains along the river and it was their wool that brought wealthy merchants into the town to trade. The handsome Woolmarket was built in 1500. Parts of the church date back to 1230. Between the church and the Woolmarket is a Gobbleshoot, a long narrow passageway where the villagers would race the Christmas turkeys. Almost opposite the church, is the inn which takes its name from the bell in the church. The inn sign shows a bell with a Latin inscription, which translated says,'

'I toll for the living
I toll for the dead
I shiver the lightning.'

It was thought that the church bell would stop the lightning striking.

Around 1908 the Bell was taken over by the Turnell family. It was this family who started the Hot Cross Bun tradition. The new landlord took over the inn one Good Friday and hung a bun up in the bar. The landlords have continued with this practise every year. During the war, when the ingredients were too precious to waste, a bun made of concrete was used. By tradition the bun is hung by the oldest member of the village. For many years this was done by the same gentleman who lived to be well over a hundred, on his hundredth birthday he was presented with his own bun carved out of wood.

The Bell has been run by the Bonson family for many years. They took over in 1938 when there was no electricity, and water was drawn from a well in the courtyard. The present owner's mother-in-law Jo Bonson ran it during the last war, she also ran the only taxi in the village which she also used to pull the auxilliary pump. She looked after the twenty-five officers billeted at the Bell and many refugees who, made homeless by the German bombs, were given temporary shelter in the nearby hall. This amazing lady was also in charge of gas masks. It was her job to make sure everyone in the village, possessed one and knew how to use it. This caused many problems with the older men in the village whose magnificent beards she had great difficulty in pushing into the confined space of the gas mask.

The outside of the inn is bright with flowers. The inside is cosy and bustling with activity, even so, the staff are never too busy to be courteous, friendly and helpful. In 2001, the licensee John Vereker was unanimously voted winner of the coveted '*Pub Operator of the Year.*' It is no surprise that the Bell has won so many awards including *'Best Free House of the Year,'* and *'Best Pub in Britain'* to name but two.

LEIGH ON SEA

The Crooked Billet.

The Crooked Billet with its attractive frontage decked with flowers and hanging baskets is probably the most photographed of Old Leigh's inns. The two small cosy bars warmed by coal fires in the winter cannot contain the hundreds of visitors who crowd into the Old Town on a summer evening. They overflow onto the nearby wharf where they can drink their pint, buy fresh cockles and watch the boats bringing in and unloading their catch. The outside rendering on the Crooked Billet covers a timber framed building built in the sixteenth century. Originally there was a large room at the rear but this was demolished to make way for the railway.

No one is sure where the name comes from. A billet is a piece of wood. The inn sign shows an old fisherman walking with the aid of a crooked walking stick. It could be that the name came from the seamen's billet or workhouse. Opposite the Crooked Billet on the other side of the railway is Billet Lane, once known as Workhouse Lane after the workhouse built there by Richard Haddock the famous Leigh sea captain. On the corner of Workhouse Lane was once an old timbered beerhouse called The Billet. This was the house where Richard Haddock and his son were born. Captain Haddock sold the House in 1707. It ceased to be a beerhouse and the licence was given to the Coal Hole, almost opposite the Crooked Billet and now used as a Sea Scout headquarters

Many pubs organised some kind of group or club or benevolent society and the Billet was no exception. The Fishermen's Club' sometimes called the Billet Club or the United Bretheren was held there from 1853. The club was for fishermen only. Members had to live within a mile of the Billet. Every year the members were invited to the rectory for dinner. After dinner they danced on the rectory lawn. The servants kept them well supplied with beer.

This was obviously a highly successful party, for the fishermen always took the next week off!

The Peter Boat

Further along the High Street, is the 17th century Peter Boat public house. The present car park once housed four shops, several cottages, stables and a slaughterhouse. Situated right on the waterfront it was an ideal place for the Leigh smugglers. A large secret underground room directly connected to the waterside was built to store the contraband. Horses were kept in the stables in nearby Alley Dock, these were used to take the contraband along a small path beside the inn, across country to Daws Heath, a lonely and lawless place. Here grew a huge elm tree, known as Adams Elm. The tree, thirty foot in circumference was hollow, and made the perfect hiding place for the smuggled goods until they could be collected and moved on.

Next door to the Peter Boat lived Elizabeth Little. Around 1884 she owned a small draper's shop. She sold silk, lace, perfume, gin, brandy and rum, all illegally obtained goods. Elizabeth was as good a sailor as the men. She was also as competent a smuggler.

Once a coastguard cutter patrolling the Essex coast fired a shot across the bows of her boat. Elizabeth put on more sail and tried to make a run for it. The coastguards fired again this time wounding her young brother Bon. Elizabeth headed for Barling creek, she knew the water here was too shallow for the cutter to follow. She unloaded Bon and the contraband and sailed the empty boat back to Leigh. She sent someone up to Wakering Church to fetch Benniworth the undertaker. Together they hid the booty under the floor of the hearse, put Bon in the coffin and drove home. Elizabeth, wrapped in a black shawl looked every bit the grieving widow. Even the customs men raised their hats to the coffin as it passed.

The Cotgroves were also a well known smuggling family.

Charles was once caught and taken to Chelmsford jail. He swore he had found the barrel of drink floating on the water and rescued it thinking it had come from a wreck and he hadn't had time to declare it before he was stopped by the custom's man. He had in fact threatened to throw the customs man overboard.

One night, a shipload of contraband was landed, taken to the Peter Boat and hidden in the secret underground passageway. The landlord and his brother, pleased that the task of stowing away the goods was safely finished, were going up the stairs when one of them tripped and dropped the lamp. Immediately the stairs were ablaze.

In no time the timber framed inn was engulfed in flames. The Leigh men rushed to Alley Dock to dam the creek and trap the tide. They formed a chain, passing buckets up and down in a desperate effort to save the inn. Alas they were too late. The inn burned to the ground, revealing the secret cellar and its contents.

The men's club which met at the Peter Boat had a hundred and fifty members. They called themselves the Comical Fellows on account of their bizarre way of dressing for meetings. Each year they met at the Peter Boat for a great celebration, the best London entertainers were booked, the best food was eaten and copious wine and ale was drunk. These meetings became so expensive that the funds ran out. Subscriptions had to be increased. This was not a popular move and many members left. The Comicals gradually ceased to exist. They, like the other men's clubs in the Old town, were invited by Cannon King to a church service and afterwards a feast at the rectory.

The inn takes its name from the Peter Boat a clinker built boat, predecessor of the bawley which in turn took its name from the boiler which was fitted on the boat to boil the shrimps and cockles.

The Smack

The Smack was originally on the North side of the High street opposite Junipers shop. But when the railway was planned the Smack was right in the middle of its path and had to be demolished. It was rebuilt in its present position which had been a coal yard and storage area next to Junipers which is said to have been where John Constable the famous Essex painter lived for a time.

Craddock who bought the old brick farmhouse later named Lapwater Hall, stayed at the Smack while he was waiting for repairs to be done on his house. He also stabled his horse there. The horse with no ears which he used on his many highway robberies.

The Smack has had many owners. In 1839 Samuel Fairchild was the licensee, by 1845 John Bayford lived there with his wife, seven children, his sister, a servant and one lodger. In 1861 it was listed as the Smack and Railway Tavern.

In 1874 John Bundock is named as the landlord.

It is still very pleasant to have a meal sitting practically on the river, in the back room of the Smack. But the prices today are a little different from those of 1963 when the following was served:-
Mulligatawny soup 1s.6d. (8p)
Halibut 8s.6d. (48p)
Rump steak 12s.6d. (63p)
Raspberries and cream, 3s.6d. (18p)
Coffee 2s. (10p)
Bottle Mateus rose 18s.6d. (93p)
Meal for four and wine £4.10s. (£4.50)
The sign hanging outside the pub depicts a smack, a single masted sailing boat used for fishing.

The Ship

The sign outside the Ship, on the other side of the railway, almost opposite the Smack, shows a much grander vessel. The old sign has been replaced during the recent change of management.

About twenty years ago, a couple, regulars at the Ship, had done a favour for the landlord who was so grateful that he said: "You can have anything in this pub in return." Having had a good few drinks they replied: "We'll have those" pointing to two of the lovely etched glass windows. The next day there were the windows, removed from their frames, waiting for them. They were completely taken aback but not wishing to offend they took the windows home.

During the recent refurbishment a lady walked into the bar carrying two etched glass panels. Apparently they had lain unwanted in their garage for the twenty years. Noticing the decorating she decided to return them and they have now been restored to their original place behind the bar.

The present day Ship was built on the site of a much earlier inn. Originally a private house belonging to Thomas Stevens. In 1773 it was granted the licence held by the George when the George became a private house. Behind the Ship was Eden Lodge where Mrs Thackeray the novelist's wife lived for a time. There was also an old beer distillery and piece of land known as Beacon Field, presumably where the fire beacon was situated.

The Forresters met at the Ship. Once a year the men would be invited to the rectory. First they marched up the hill to the church for a service and then on to the vicarage where Canon King gave them a slap up dinner.

The Sarah Moore

The Sarah Moore, up the hill from the Old Town, opened to the public in the summer of 2000. Named after Sarah Moore the famous witch of Leigh. Sarah is reputed to have put curses on many of the locals in her time. Once when a woman refused to give her money she put a curse of the hare lip on her unborn child and all subsequent children in the family. She was also blamed for the death of a child she caught in her house on the Strand Warf in Old Leigh. The children were snooping in Sarah's house when Sarah came in and caught them. One small boy, terrified at being caught dropped the candle he was holding. He was immediately engulfed in flames. There is some doubt about whether Sarah was trying to put out the flames or if she actually caused his death from sparks that came out of her eyes. It was Sarah who put curses on the fishermen if they failed to toss her a coin. This proved to be her undoing for one ship's skipper refused to pay for a fair wind from Sarah and was caught in a terrible storm. The crew were convinced it was Sarah's doing. The Skipper grabbed and axe and chopped three great blows to the bow of the ship. Immediately the storm ceased its raging. When they returned to the quay the fishermen found Sarah dead, with three gashes in her head.

On opening day one of the inn's employees dressed up as the old witch, whose picture had been reproduced for the inn sign.

The Carlton

The Carlton began life as a coaching Inn. The London to Southend Coaching Company used to stable their horses there. The Carlton was first granted a liquor licence in 1896.

Men working on the Carlton found a dog which had been buried in the wall. This was often done and was supposed to be a good luck charm and also to help repel evil spirits. Leigh was for years the home of several well known witches. Just a short distance away is the Doom Pond where witches were ducked. A rope would be tied round the unfortunate woman's waist and she was pushed into the pond. If she floated she must surely be a witch. If she sank and drowned she was not guilty. A case of damned if she is and damned if she isn't.

The Elms

The Elms building was originally a farmhouse known as Elm Farm. Named after the great Elm tree which stood close by. The enormous elm gradually decayed, and became just a hollow shell, so big that twelve men could stand inside it. No other elm tree would grow in its place. The farm had many names, Adams Elm, Allen's Elm, Ellen Elm Farm. The present day pub includes part of the original building which is mainly mid-nineteenth century. It belonged to the Webb family who were a well known Leigh farming family. To begin with, William worked incognito at Elm Farms as a ploughman. When the farm came on the market about 1780 he went to the auction and bought it for £800.

William Webb died in 1793. His son John died after being kicked by a horse and the farm passed to his widow Elizabeth. In 1856 the farmhouse and its fifty three acres of land were put up for auction.

It had several owners until 1881 when it was bought for £2,100 by Thomas Smith a wealthy coal merchant from Kent. Smith sold the house and part of the farm land plus Leigh Hall and its farm to Frederick Ramuz, a property developer and speculator who became Mayor of Southend. Ramuz divided the land into small building plots and called it Leigh Hall Estate. The estate was advertised as *'the New Eldorado.'* Plots were auctioned from a marquee on the site. The farmhouse was bought by Henry King who leased it to George Mills of Leigh. This was in 1900. Mills was acting on behalf of Ramuz who provided the money but wanted to remain anonymous. Mills applied for and was granted a licence to sell wines, beers and spirits. He turned the house into The Elms Inn or Public House. He stipulated that on completion of the work when the pub opened in 1900 Ramuz would employ him as its manager and pay him a salary of £2 a week.

In the 1920s workmen found a bottle under the floorboards of the Elms. In it was an account written by Lawrence Davis who had once farmed there for twenty years. He tells of his terribly hard life and how he could never make a profit. The farm was very inconvenient, the dairy, facing east had the sun from early morning shining on the milk pans. He mentions that a two-acre field was sold for £60 and was to be used as a cemetery on the road to Hadleigh. He kept three horses and no less than six cows. He built a cottage for his labourer who could neither read nor write and belonged to a sect called the Peculiar People. Later he mentions the labourer's wife had become a lady and would not do a thing. Her husband earned 15 shillings a week and house and wood free. At harvest he had £8 to £9 and a barrel of beer and supper. Davis paid £120 a year rent, never made a shilling profit. The worst years were 1875 to 80 when there was great competition from America.. He mentions the harvest being ruined by constant rain and the dear Rev. King returning ten per cent of the tithe money.

He ends with:
'Adieu should you read this within 100 years, please bury it again in some dry part of the Elm building.
faithfully yours,
Lawrence Davis'

The Elms became a well known landmark in Leigh. All the land between Hadleigh and the Elms at one time belonged to the Salvation Army and no pub was allowed to be built there. At one time it was a principle coach and bus stop. It was also a well known stopping place for horses, the horse trough stood outside. At one time the name was changed. This caused such consternation amongst the locals that the name had to be changed back to the Elms.

MALDON

The Blue Boar

Situated right in the centre of the High Street in historic Maldon, is the Blue Boar. The design pictured on the inn sign was the symbol of the great and powerful de Vere family of Oxford. Their home was quite near, at Hedingham. One of the de Vere's retainers was given the house which he converted into an inn and gave it the badge of his former employer. The Blue Boar is very ancient. The lounge and part of the dining room date back to 1390. It has been an inn since 1593 when it was known as Blewe Bore. Accounts from All Saint's Church for 1573 reads:

> *to the Dean of Westminster, 1 gallon of wine and 1lb Sugar at his dinner at the Blewe Bore 3s 8d.*
> *13d Mr Simpson's horsemeat at the Blewe Bore when he preached on Bartholomew day.*

In 1957 a boar's head was cooked at the Blue Boar Maldon then flown to New York. It was cooked according to an ancient recipe from six hundred years ago. The boar's head was the main feature of a great feast organised by a group named 'Neighbours United' which was an organisation dedicated to fight juvenile crime. The head was escorted from the airport to the restaurant by mummers dressed in costume as part of a torchlight procession.

In 1769 the Blue Boar was registered to a William May. By 1861 Ann Lansdell ran it, helped by her daughter and two servants. The 1871 census shows William Hickford in charge. He was also agent for the Great Eastern Railway. His wife, a nephew, a cook, a maid and a boots helped with the running of the inn. It was run by Trust Houses Ltd in 1925.

PAGLESHAM

The Punch Bowl

The rather elegant three storey white weather boarded Punch Bowl at Church End Paglesham was, until the mid-eighteenth century, known as the Blue House. The original Punch Bowl was situated between the school and the church. It's position, on the edge of the desolate saltings made Paglesham an ideal spot for smugglers. At one time nearly everyone in the village had some part in that illegal trade. Three elm pollards in the area were a favourite hiding place. At times hundreds of pounds worth of silks and spirits would be hidden in the hollow trunks. Many of the houses had secret compartments to hide the contraband. One cottage was known as 'The Smugglers Hoard.' At Paglesham the trade was usually in wool, brandy and Geneva. 13,476 gallons were imported in one year. Locals said at the time that Paglesham was awash with gin. In fact they were supposed to have used gin to clean their windows. Smuggling made many men in the area very rich. No one was above taking advantage of the trade, even the local Magistrates sent their servants out to collect their share of the goods.

A John Dowsett owned a cutter named Big Jane. She was armed with six brass guns. Big Jane was involved in several disputes with the government ships. Dowsett's son-in-law, William Blythe, known as 'Hard Apple' had many a run in with the revenue men. Once when he was boarded by the revenue men Blythe offered to surrender so many barrels. The barrels were loaded onto the customs boat. Blythe was generously passing glasses of wine to the officers and crew, who became more and more under the influence, and failed to notice that as soon as a barrel was put on board their vessel it was taken off and returned to the cutter.

Another time Blythe saved the customs vessel from going

aground and at the same time saved himself from being hanged.

The village cricket matches took place outside the Punch Bowl. The players laid down their jackets and left their loaded pistols and cutlasses handy, just in case of trouble, and the game would begin. There is a tale of the day the team arrived to play cricket in the field by the Punchbowl when they found a bull which had terrorised the neighbourhood, standing on the pitch. The animal charged. Blyth being a member of the team, was having no nonsense.

"Body and Bones" he shouted *"don't think to frighten me."* Then he grabbed the bull by its tail and beat the poor beast with a stick. The bull rushed off across the field, jumping over a hedge and a ditch with Blyth still holding onto its tail. Eventually the bull, from exhaustion and fright, dropped dead. Hard Apple was indeed a strange character. He once drank two glasses of wine and then ate the glasses with no ill effect. He died in 1830.

It was in the Punch Bowl that the cricket club held its dinners and the locals their harvest suppers. A little further along the road, by the church is Worlds End Cottage, which was at one time an ale house run by James Paine.

The Punch Bowl, bright with containers of flowers, nestles amongst the delightful cottages at Church End Paglesham.

The Plough & Sail

The village is divided into two separate parts, Church End and East End.

The attractive weather-boarded Plough and Sail is at East End, just yards away from the River Crouch. Over five hundred years old, the inn has always played an important part in life in the village. The village fairs were held in the open space around the inn.

In the 1841 census George Fairchild lived there with his wife Henrietta and their four children. At a sale of the property it was described as having a ninety-seven foot frontage and accommodation consisting of a parlour, keeping room, pantry, taproom bar, four bedrooms and a cellar. There were several outbuildings behind the inn, including a two piggeries, a ten-pin bowling shed and a bakehouse with an oven. The oven was used by anyone from the village. They could cook their Sunday roast, bread and pies, for just one penny.

PELDON

The Rose

The Rose at Peldon was first registered as an inn in 1454, but it was built earlier, probably in the thirteenth century. Next to the inn is the village pond which is mentioned in the Doomsday Book. Like many an Essex inn the Peldon Rose was ideally suited for the smuggler, situated as it is near the desolate mudflats close to the mouth of the River Blackwater.

Smuggling began in England when Edward II levied a tax on foreign wines. This led to huge amounts of wines and spirits being smuggled into the country. Much of the trade was carried out by quite unsavoury villains and pirates who thought nothing of killing anyone who got in their way. They made vast fortunes out of the contraband goods which were shipped into the main ports of London, Bristol and Liverpool. It was a hazardous profession involving a great deal of risk. Smuggling on a smaller scale thrived in most coastal towns and villages. The goods, carefully packed in waterproof barrels, would be thrown over the side of a larger ship close to the shore. The local fishermen would sail silently into tiny creeks and inlets pick up the goods, almost under the nose of the customs man. (Frequently even with their co-operation.) Then they would quietly return home, safe in the knowledge that the custom's boats were too big to follow them through the little shallow creeks.

Most coastal taverns relied on bootlegged wine, gin, brandy, and rum which was usually in Ankers, wooden barrels containing about eight gallons. The local inn was an obvious place to store smuggled goods and they often had a secret tunnel or room specially built for the purpose. The Peldon Rose was no exception, standing by itself on the lonely road to Mersea Island with its intricate creeks and mudflats. Right beside the inn is the pond with a deep well inside.

Mrs Pullen whose family ran the inn from around 1881 until 1933 can remember as a child lying in bed and hearing barrels being rolled down the road at dead of night to the pond and lowered into the well on thick ropes. The landlord's reward for the risk of storing the goods was a fair share of bootleg rum, Geneva from Holland, cognac and wines from France, chewing tobacco laced with molasses. These goods plus ribbons, tea, cloth and gold were extremely lucrative and often taken to be sold in Chelmsford and other large towns.

Rev. Baring Gould was Rector of East Mersea for ten years from 1871 to 1881. He disliked living on the island but it was there that he wrote his famous book Mehalah. The heroine, a wild beautiful gypsy girl who lived on nearby Ray Island was often to be seen rowing her little dinghy across to the Rose Inn.

In the great earthquake that shook many parts of Essex in 1884, the Peldon Rose was quite badly shaken. A chimney fell down, cracks appeared in walls and part of the roof was badly damaged, the nearby church was also a victim of the quake.

ROCHFORD

The King's Head.

The ancient King's Head was called the Blue Boar until around 1793. At that time the coach started at the Blue Boar and travelled to Rayleigh, Billericay and on to Shenfield. A few years later a stage coach and a diligence, a kind of continental style coach, made the journey three times a week, through Ironwell Lane and on to London. The fare was eight shillings.

It was at the King's Head that the feast, which took place before the famous Whispering Court, was held. The King's Court, known as the Whispering or Lawless or Cockcrowing Court has been held for hundreds of years but the existing roll of stewards goes back only to 1758. The Little Lawless court was held on Rope Monday, which was the second Monday after Easter. The Great Lawless Court on the Wednesday before the feast of St Michael at the end of September. The court originated from the time when the Lord of the Manor returning home late one night overheard some of his tenant farmers plotting against him. He ordered all the tenants of his Manor to assemble at a certain hour, on the same spot at Rayleigh where the conspirators had met, and do homage for their lands. The court was originally held at Kings Hill, Rayleigh but was transferred to Rochford by the second Earl of Warwick because, *"He would have it so."*

The supper at the King's Head was a lavish affair. Between ten and fifteen men attended. The meal consisted of boiled fowls, a boiled leg of mutton, with caper sauce, vegetables, ale, plum pudding, apple tarts and sweets. After supper a large bowl of punch was served with a silver ladle containing a coin of King George II. Pipes and tobacco were introduced, then another bowl and again another.

This steaming punch was made of rum, brandy, port, sherry,

shrub, spruce, hot water, lemon and sugar galore. They toasted the Queen, and then began the revelry. Songs were sung and hilarity prevailed. They marched to the whispering post which is first mentioned in the steward's rolls in 1772. The second post which is still in existence was erected in 1867 and made of wood exactly like the former, about five feet high, the top is spike shaped to represent the flame of a candle.

It was etiquette that no one but the chairman should consult his watch, soon after midnight he quietly rose, put on his hat and coat opened the door and stood a few minutes as if listening for the cock to crow. The guests followed his example. At some secret signal a man appeared, carrying across his shoulder a heavy stake or fire brand blazing for a foot and a half of its length. Then others appeared carrying links (a torch of pitch and tow) they followed the steward in procession along the street. Through a crowd of lads cock crowing with all their might.

When they arrived at the place of penance, the tenants kneeled around the white pillar. Then the steward in a whisper said,

"*O Yes, O yes, O yes, all manner of persons that do owe suit and service to this court now to be holden in and for the manner of Kings Hill in the hundred of Rochford, draw near and give your attendance.*"

Then he called the names of each tenant who replied

"*Here Sir.*"

Anyone who did not reply was fined for every hour he was absent. The firebrands were extinguished at the foot of the post. Out of the embers a piece was taken to mark a tally for attendance and rent. The link bearers rushed forward and beat their torches against the post to extinguish them. (This was forbidden by the steward.) The onlookers' shouts of cock-a-whoops arose in all keys. The members of the court then returned by a different route to the Kings Head, where if a licence has been obtained another bowl of punch was waiting for them. The minutes of the court were originally written with charcoal. The rents produced about £6, which hardly paid for the supper.

The Old Ship

Records for the Old Ship go back as far as 1670, when Edward Paine was the landlord. It is however probably much older than that. It was sold to Dorothy Atkinson in the *'two and fortieth year of Elizabeth 1st.'* At one time there was a butcher's shop in the yard at the back of the premises. This was owned by Thomas Fairhead. He and his friend Henry Gilliot, who was a shepherd at Prittlewell, were not above a spot of dishonest business. Eventually they were caught, tried, and hanged on the scaffold at Moulsham Street, Chelmsford. They were the last men in England to be hanged for sheep and cow stealing.

Mary, the landlord's young daughter was engaged to Thomas Fairhead. She was devastated at his death and died a short time afterwards. People said she died of a broken heart. Fairhead was a fine young man from a very respectable family of Rayleigh. Several of the family had been church wardens. People thought that he had been led astray by Gilliot, who at his trial wanted it known that it was his fault that the others had participated in the crimes. Gilliot left a wife to whom he had been married for just one month. Gilliot and Fairhead were twenty-four years old. Henry Jay was convicted with them, he was younger and sentenced to be transported.

The Old Ship was a favourite with the many fairground people who came to the market square. There were special rings attached to the outside wall, for them to tie up their performing bears while they went inside for a pint. The room upstairs was used by the True Friendship Masonic Lodge and was more recently the meeting place of the Rochford Music Club.

The New Ship

Behind the Old Ship is the New Ship, paradoxically older than the Old Ship. Legend says that there were two brothers in Rochford, one bought the Ship. His brother was angry about this and out of spite opened a rival establishment which he named the New Ship. There is some doubt about this. It is also suggested it gained its name from the new ships which were built in the nearby shipyard.

Along with many inns the New Ship was the Headquarters for some rather strange clubs. One of these at the New Ship was the 'Rochford Hundred Association Against Murderers, Felons and Thieves etc.' Anyone in the Rochford hundred could join. Membership was ten shillings and sixpence. A committee member had to pay fifteen shillings. They met every Thursday afternoon and anyone failing to attend had to pay sixpence towards the expenses of those who did attend. The association was prepared to meet all reasonable expenses caused by the apprehending and prosecuting of offenders. The aim of the Association was to suppress crime and protect the property of its members. Members were rewarded for bringing criminals to justice. The reward for bringing to justice anyone guilty of wilful murder was £10, housebreakers, £10. Anyone setting fire to barn, haystack, corn or house £10. Stealing or maliciously killing a member's horse £10, forgery £5. Catching a highwayman or footpad £5. Catching anyone maiming a sheep or cow, ox or bull £5. Poachers £5.

The Golden Lion

The attractive beamed building dates back to the sixteenth century. It was once a tailor's shop. It became an alehouse known as the Red Lion, and was licensed to sell beer, sherry and cider. Formerly for some years it was known as Harris and Locks tenement.

The Golden Lion belonged to the Pettigrew family for many years. The inn has changed a little over the years, the two bars have been knocked into one large bright room. A picture of Mrs Pettigrew serving behind the bar hangs on the wall The picture was probably taken in the thirties, it shows how little the bar has changed in that time. The well discovered in the back yard which once served all the neighbouring properties has been filled in.

The Horse & Groom

The Horse and Groom once stood on the edge of the brook beside Salt Bridge. The original inn is now the tack room, a Grade II listed building. Although officially in the parish of Eastwood the Horse and Groom played an important part in Rochford life. It was there that the Bailiff of the Manor of Rochford collected rents from the Eastwood parish. When all the tithes were paid, a great meal of pigeon pie was enjoyed by the tenants. The pigeons would be from the huge dovecote at nearby Rochford Hall. Courtesy of the local shepherd who tucked them in his greatcoat pocket and carried them secretly to the inn.

The present inn is built at right angles to the original building. Being so close to the River Roach, the Horse and Groom has always suffered from flooding. Flooding occurred as recently as the year 2000 when the public house was closed several times due to flooding during the torrential rain.

The Marlborough Head

The Marlborough Head is one of Rochford's oldest and most attractive pubs. It is named after the Duke of Marlborough (1650-1722) a great military leader. His victory at Blenheim resulted in the building of Blenheim Palace.

Benton the great Essex Historian tells that the Marlborogh had many hardened drinkers as customers. The farmers of the area, who were great drinkers used to go to the Marlborough. They would take with them a hen and they refused to leave until the hen had incubated her eggs.

It is thought that Wellington's Officers were billeted at the Marlborough. It was connected by many tunnels to the nearby buildings in Barrack Lane. Like so many inns the Marlborough has a ghost which has been seen and heard on many occasions.

SHOEBURYNESS

The Captain Mannering.

Once part of the Shoebury Barracks. The name is taken from Dad's Army, the famous TV programme starring Arthur Lowe as the pompous Captain Mainwaring. It is his picture on the inn sign.

The property was built in 1898 as a hospital for dependants of military families of non-commissioned ranks, serving at Shoebury Garrison. It was erected as a memorial to seven men killed in an accident on the ranges in 1885. The army was carrying out experimental firing of a new type of shell. One morning in February 1885 one of the fuses failed and the shell refused to fire. Sergeant Major Daykin tried to shift the fuse with a hammer. The six inch, hundred pound bomb exploded, killing Sergeant Major Daykin, two Colonels, a Captain and two gunners. Four other men were badly injured. Queen Victoria sent messages of condolences. The town closed on the day of their funeral as a tribute to the men. A plaque to their memory was placed in the Garrison Church.

The building has had many alterations and been extended over the years. Bathrooms and indoor toilets have been added. In 1909 extra living quarters were provided for the nurses. It remained a Hospital until the 1947 National Health Act. From then until 1960 it was a hostel for married families and at one time it was a YMCA. The ivy-covered building was last used in 1976 and the building became neglected. It was given a new lease of life and is now a fascinating reminder of the Army presence in Shoebury. Memorabilia adorns the walls, uniforms, rifles, a map of the Western Front, and notices such as *'Hitler will send no warning, so always carry your gas mask.'*

STAPLEFORD TAWNEY

The Mole Trap

The Mole Trap must be one of the most attractive inns in the county. It is thought to be the only pub named The Mole Trap. The name came about when Joseph Threader invented a trap for catching moles. It sold so well that with the proceeds he bought the house and named it the Mole Trap.

After his death his wife Rebecca carried on the business. Their only son died before Rebecca, who lived to be over ninety. Joseph's grandson Sam took over the inn but never married. His sister remembers with affection the time when the tiny tap room was the meeting place for the villagers.

Many a sing-song took place there. All around the bar were wooden seats. Next to the brick fireplace there used to be a round hole with small drawer underneath. This was where the locals played pitch penny with coins worn smooth with use. Drawn on one of the tables was a shove ha'penny board. Another game played at the time was Toad-in-the-Hole. The men tried to throw brass discs into a hole in a bench. Sadly the discs were stolen during the First World War.

On fine days the men would take their pewter tankards out to the nearby meadow to play quoits. The Mole Trap was open all day every day except Sunday. Even on Sunday anyone who could prove they had come more than three miles was served.

When Sam died, his brother John took over. The inn was in the Threader family for around twenty-five years. During alterations a little book was discovered with details of various jobs carried out over the last 200 years.

Set in the heart of the countryside, surrounded by fields, the attractive little pub in the back of beyond may once have had the distinction of being the smallest pub in Essex. That was before the small dining room was added. In front of the Mole Trap is a pretty garden where chickens wander with the occasional duck from the nearby pond.

Across the fields you may be lucky enough to catch sight of a group of deer ambling along the horizon.

STOCK

The Bear

The Bear Inn at Stock was bought by the Wake family in the fifteenth century. It was named the Bear in memory of "the Great White Bear", "God's Dog" or "the old man in the fur coat". A huge bear killed by a single blow of the sword by their ancestor Herewood the Wake, while he was visiting his uncle's castle.

When the Roundheads took power in England they demanded that many inns were to be closed. Somehow the Bear was left open but its name had to be changed. The landlord, tongue in cheek renamed it 'The Brew Inn' (bruin being the French word for bear.) The Bear, was a stopping place for coaches travelling from London to Chelmsford.

The Bear has one unique tale, the story of Spider Marshall. Spider was a man of uncouth habits and strange mannerisms. It was his curious sideways scuttling walk that earned him the name Spider. His main job was to look after the horses of visitors to the inn. A small rather shrewd and cunning man he was always on the lookout for ways of making a little extra money. When strangers visited the inn Spider would perform one of his favourite tricks. He would shin up the chimney in the taproom and magically appear in the bar parlour. The chimneys met and he could go up one and down the other at will. This trick usually earned him a drink or two. Where the chimneys met was a small space, probably used for smoking bacon. This is where Spider would sit, sometimes for hours, refusing to come down. The locals would smoke him out by pushing burning straw into the fireplace and up the chimney. His strange behaviour proved to be Spider's undoing. One Christmas Eve after partaking of a good few pints, he climbed up to the bacon loft for the last time. It was assumed he suffocated there. Spider's ghost has been seen on several occasions wandering through the bar. He became quite a celebrity. At one time a 'Spider Marshall Club' was formed in his memory.

The Cock

The Cock was first mentioned in 1519 but it is thought to be much older than this. One of the earliest references to the Cock is in John Ponder's will in 1527. He bequeathes to his 'dowter a feather bed, that is at the sygne of cokk.' In those days this would have been a much prized possession. The will goes on to say that nothing shall be taken out of the house 'called cokk yn Stoke' it shall be sold after my life if I do not sell it in my life. Two witnesses, John Freeman and John Stoward Turner of Buttsbury read the will on the 'III day off March' in the back yard of the Cock.

There is a tale that at one time a stranger arrived at the Cock and was having a drink in the tap room when much to the dismay of those present he collapsed and died. This caused a rather bizarre situation for the parish boundary went right through the middle of the tap room, had he died in Stock or Buttsbury? Finally after much deliberation it was decided that the parish where his head was lying would be the parish to bury him. It could be that the unfortunate victim was displeased with this decision for he is still haunting the tap room.

In the early sixties the Cock had a table made from a huge pair of bellows from the nearby smithy when it closed down. There was also a polyphon a giant antique musical box which cost one penny to operate. It was a primitive juke box made in Germany.

At that time a three course lunch at the Cock cost 7s.6d. (37p) and a bottle of wine cost 13s.6d. (67p)

TILBURY

The World's End

Tilbury is best known for its fort, docks and the Tilbury Ferry. Until comparatively recently a car ferry ran from Tilbury to Gravesend. The ferry was there long long ago, possibly as far back as Roman times. In the thirteenth century it was used by Pilgrims on their way to Canterbury. There is a story that Charles I once crossed over on the ferry accompanied by the Marquis of Buckingham and an aide. All three were in disguise. They paid the ferryman with a gold coin, a fortune in those days. The ferryman thought this was very suspicious and called the military. When they arrived, Lord Buckingham removed his false beard and to their horror, they realised they had arrested the Lord Admiral.

Henry IV granted Tilbury the rights of ferry as compensation to the town for the damage done by French pirates. In the early seventeenth century the nearby Tilbury Fort became more or less deserted. No one lived there except the master-gunner who kept a victualling house for the fishermen. The inn was the residence of the Governor of Tilbury Fort in the mid seventeenth century. His pay apparently was so much in arrears that he was allowed to run the ferry and the inn. Many of the rich and famous have stayed at the World's End. Samuel Pepys stayed for a time and Nick Nevenson the notorious highwayman, and Daniel Defoe, author of Moll Flanders and Robinson Crusoe. Defoe once owned a tile factory across the river at Dartford.

The World's end was rebuilt in 1788. In 1840 William Creed kept the alehouse then known as the Ferry House. The Ferry House has had many names over the years. In 1769 it was known as the Suttling house. Suttlers sold food to the soldiers, it comes from an old Dutch word meaning 'to perform mean duties.' The present name the

World's End is very apt for it stands in lonely isolation by the desolate sea wall.

In 1880 The London to Southend railway acquired the ancient ferry or water passage across the Thames from Tilbury to Gravesend from the trustees of the will of Thomas Cheeseman. The Secretary of State agreed to grant the lease to W. Chadwell. With the ferry went the ferry house known as the World's End, the causeway or landing place, stabling, a barn, coach house, open shed and outbuildings and plots of land adjoining the Ferry House. Officers were to be allowed free passage across the river with or without field guns, carriages baggage, wives or children, between the hours of seven in the morning and seven at night. Non-commissioned officers and privates or women were to pay two pence, children one penny, field guns and carriages one shilling per wheel, horses one shilling and baggage five shillings a ton.

The Ferry House had to be maintained in good order, along with the house and drains, ditches and fences. The property could be inspected by the Secretary of State or his officers. Outside the inn is still a large mounting block a reminder of the time when the horse was the only means of transport.

WAKERING

The Castle Inn

1782 John Monk took over as landlord of the Castle Inn. A few years later he married Elizabeth, daughter of Thomas Blencowe of Trotters farm. For several years, as well as being the innkeeper, John was the village constable. Also, on the quiet he was, if not a smuggler, certainly a receiver of ill-gotten gains.

This was quite a boost to the takings of the inn. Nearly all inns sold smuggled goods. People greatly resented the high tax in wines and spirits and considered the customs men were fair game for any illegal adventures. For a time John was overseer of the poor, another boost to the takings, for he also kept the village store and was in charge of providing the food for the poor.

In 1814 John Monk junior took over the Castle from his father as well as the job of overseer to the poor. He married Sarah Pledger, a local farmer's daughter. They were a popular couple.

In those days Wakering was a remote and lawless place and the inn was the centre of village life. Meetings and clubs took place there. In front of the inn was a kind of shed where the village cobbler repaired shoes. He was not a popular man in the village. One night in a drunken, belligerent mood, the shoemaker started an argument with the innkeeper and insisted on going outside to fight. Reluctantly John agreed. The two men went outside to the back of the building. Behind the inn was a drainage ditch carrying away the local sewage. John stood with his back to the ditch. When the shoemaker ran and lunged at him, John neatly side-stepped and his opponent landed in amongst the sewage, causing a great deal of hilarity amongst the onlookers.

The Inn changed hands about 1823. John Wilson is recorded as the innkeeper then.

The Red Lion,

Papers found in a Southend solicitors office in the early ninteen-forties include minutes of the Great Wakering Association for the Prosecution of Murderers, Felons and Thieves etc. This was formed at the Lion in November 1834. The aim was to give legal help to members and to prosecute villains when necessary. Like many such associations the members spent a great deal of time wining and dining. At an annual dinner at the Lion Inn, for which the Treasurer *'do pay out one shilling to each member towards the expense of such dinner,'* twenty members attended and thirty-three bottles of wine were drunk.

In 1887, the fifteen members consumed
>8 bottles of hock   £2
>9 bottles of St Juliian £2 5s
>6 bottles of sherry   3s 4d
>Brandy 7s
>Whiskey 2s 6d
>Cigars 9s
>Tobacco 2s 6d
>Coffee 10s
>Desserts 9s

WALTHAM ABBEY

The Welsh Harp

The Welsh Harp in historic Waltham Abbey was originally named the Harp. The delightful building with its beams and its lopsided overhanging upper floor was built partly in the sixteenth and the seventeenth century. The more ancient part incorporates an archway which leads to the Abbey churchyard.

In the Middle Ages pilgrims would come to the Abbey to see King Harold's tomb. After his defeat at the battle of Hastings his body was brought by Edith Swanneck his love, to Waltham to be buried. A small stone shows the spot where he is thought to lie.

It was in the seventeenth century that the Harp is first recorded as an inn. During building work a paper was discovered, it acknowledged the receipt of £5, probably a quarter's rent. It was dated 1680.

The inn was known as the Harp in 1863 but is thought to have been changed to the Welsh Harp in that year. One theory is that it was changed to celebrate the twenty-first birthday of the Prince of Wales. Queen Victoria's eldest son was born in 1841 and made Prince of Wales one month after he was born. He later became King Edward VII.

There seem to be another connection with Wales, for a little pewter button was found under the floorboards. It was decorated with the Prince of Wales' feathers. The Light Dragoons, the Prince of Wales' own regiment had their headquarters at the inn during the Napoleonic wars.

Records show William Skinner was the licensee at the Harp in 1863. By 1876 he was landlord of the Welsh Harp. He lived there with his wife two daughters a servant and a potman.

WOODHAM MORTIMER

The Hurdlemaker's Arms

This delightful little pub is the only one in England that can boast the name Hurdlemaker's Arms. It began life as a farmhouse named Conduit Hall Farm. The name Hurdlemaker's Arms comes from the time when the owner of the tiny cottage which adjoined the farm was a hurdlemaker, wood dealer and beerhouse keeper. Hurdles are rectangular frames made of withies or wooden bars, used as strong frames or fences. They are woven from flexible branches of willow. Withy fences were used in horse racing. Also, frames were used to drag traitors to their execution.

    Like many public houses of the time it doubled as a house, a pub and a meeting place for the locals. Villagers would gather there to talk, do business and drink the home made ale. The oldest part of the inn was built of lath and plaster at the time of Elizabeth I.

    In 1876 the owner found himself in serious money troubles and was obliged to sell the premises to Gray's Brewery in order to pay off his debts. He continued there as a tenant for many years. It was a rather primitive life, there was no bathroom or inside toilet until 1960 when an inside bathroom was added for the use of the tenants.